THE STORY OF
SURNAMES

THE STORY OF
SURNAMES

BY

WILLIAM DODGSON BOWMAN

LONDON
GEORGE ROUTLEDGE & SONS, LTD.
BROADWAY HOUSE : 68-74 CARTER LANE, E.C.
1932

First published, February 1931
Reprinted (with a few corrections), January 1932

PRINTED IN GREAT BRITAIN BY HEADLEY BROTHERS,
109 KINGSWAY, LONDON, W.C.2 ; AND ASHFORD, KENT.

PREFACE

THE Story of Surnames is part of the history of Medieval times. It is one that makes clear, points that would otherwise be doubtful or obscure.

This popular account of surnames could not have been written if the results of the researches of Canon Bardsley, Mr. Henry Harrison and Professor Weekley had not been available and to these and others the author tenders his acknowledgments. Professor Weekley's *Romance of Names* and *Surnames* and Mr. Harrison's *Dictionary of Surnames* and Skeat's *Concise Etymological Dictionary* have proved invaluable in settling knotty points.

Among other books consulted are Bardsley, *English Surnames* (1901) ; Bardsley, *Dictionary of English and Welsh Surnames* (Oxford, 1901) ; Guppy, *Homes of Family Names in Great Britain* (1890) ; Searle, *Onomasticon Anglo-Saxonicum* (Cambridge, 1897) ; *Hundred Rolls*, 1273 ; 1275-1377 *The Letter Books* (A to F) *of the City of London* ; *London Directory* ; and for American Surnames, the *Directories* of the Cities of New York and Chicago, and *The American Language*, by H. L. Mencken.

WILLIAM DODGSON BOWMAN.

v

CONTENTS

THE STORY OF SURNAMES

CHAPTER I

INTRODUCTORY

> It was fashionable for the Clergy (especially if Regulars, Monks, or Friars) to have their *Surnames* (for Syr-names they were not) or upper names, because superadded to those given at the Font, from the places of their Nativity . . . Hence it is that in such cases we seldome charge our margin with other Authors, their *Sirname* being Author enough to avow their births therein.—T. FULLER, *Worthies of England*.

PHILOLOGISTS have been so preoccupied with other tasks in recent years, and have had so many urgent problems to solve, that it is not surprising that but few of them have done little more than take a peep into those ancient Rolls and Lists where so much ore rich in precious metal lies buried.

The story of surnames is of extraordinary fascination, for it is one in which everybody has a proprietary interest. Verstegan and Camden three centuries ago showed its importance and value, but strangely enough, it was not till the middle of the last century when Trench's *Study of Words* aroused popular interest in etymology, that surnames and their origin received any consideration. Thereafter came books and articles on the subject in sufficient number to satisfy the most voracious reader, and wild enough in their conjectures and inferences to rouse the scepticism of the most credulous. But the people of that pre-scientific age were of simple faith, and as Mr. Edwin Thomas says, were of those " who made England great, fearing neither man, nor God, nor philology."

Some of their etymologies have at least the merit of being amusing. From an issue of an influential Daily, published some forty years ago, we get that story of Mary Queen of Scots, who after being unwell at sea, tasted some marmalade for the first time and enjoyed it. After this we are gravely informed the conserve was called *Marie malade*.

The process by which a man called Anson came to be called Pawsoffski is equally ingenious. Anson equals " Hands on," which means " Paws on." From " Paws on " we get " Paws off " and thence " Pawsoffski."

If not so ludicrous many of the guesses of Lower and Ferguson, who also wrote books on English surnames, were equally inaccurate. Ferguson reversed the method used by the scientific investigator. Instead of first collecting his facts, and then generalising from them, he started off with a definite theory and sought data to support it. If the facts did not square with his preconceived idea he either ignored them or explained that fuller information on the matter had yet to turn up.

When in 1873 Canon Bardsley's *English Surnames* was published, the era of guessing and ingenious theorising came to an end. For Bardsley's work was the result of many years of patient investigation. He collected an astonishing mass of documentary evidence, not only from the early rolls, but from Church registers of a later date. His *Dictionary of English and Welsh Surnames* published in 1901 after his death contains a vast store of information invaluable to philologists. There are many inaccuracies in this but it should be remembered by the critical that Bardsley was a pioneer investigator ; and that the rough notes from which his Dictionary was compiled, were put into book form without revision.

Bardsley's successor, Professor Weekley, is the greatest English authority on this branch of philology. He has raised it to the dignity of an exact science, and his brilliant works *Romance of Names* and *Surnames* make all students of philology eager to see that Dictionary of Surnames he has so long promised them.

From the study of surnames we learn much about the people of the Middle Ages, that would otherwise remain shadowy and obscure. Through it the revealing light of history is turned, not on the whims of monarchs and intrigues of statesmen, but on the intimate and personal affairs of our forefathers in by-gone centuries. It discloses their fears and superstitions, their loves and hates, their occupations and habits. It introduces us to a primitive society when men lived closer to nature, and maintained a hand to hand struggle with the beasts of the wild. We meet the spearman, the biller, the clayer, the fletcher, and a host of others whose callings are strange. But more important still, we pull aside the veil a little that hides the past and witness the fairs and festivals of these people of long ago, listen to their strange oaths and uncouth expressions, and discover their follies and frailties.

In order to understand how we got our Surnames it is necessary to consider the conditions prevailing in England after the Conquest. In the centuries following that event hordes of priests, traders and adventurers flocked to this country from France and the Low Countries. The feudal system established by the Normans profoundly changed social and economic conditions. The great estates were held by foreigners who despised the natives and their language. A third of the land was owned by the Church, and the religious houses which sprang up everywhere were peopled by French and Italian monks.

English speech was represented by many dialects, the chief of which were the Northern, used in Northumberland, Durham, Yorkshire and the Lowlands of Scotland ; the Midland spoken in East Anglia and in the Midlands as far south as the Thames ; and the Southern dialect, the language of the people of Somersetshire, Gloucestershire, Herefordshire and in all counties south of the Thames.

Though these dialects had much in common they were yet so different that even in Caxton's time the Kentish man found it difficult to make himself understood by the Northumbrian. The coming of the Norman added to this babel-like confusion. The language of Court and the nobility was French. Boys in the grammar schools were taught Latin through the medium of French, which was also the language of the

Courts of Justice and polite society. Until the fourteenth century it was the fashionable tongue and those who desired to stand well with the ruling powers, or were ambitious, took pains to learn and speak it. As John de Trevisa, a writer of the fourteenth century, quaintly says in his translation of Higden's *Polychronicon*, " *uplondysche men wol lykne to gentile men fondeth with gret bysynes for to spake Freynsch for to be more ytold of.*"

In addition to French and the English dialects, Gaelic, Manx, Cornish, and Welsh, spoken in the outlying parts of the kingdom, added to the confusion. Instead of becoming a bi-lingual or tri-lingual nation, the English people clung obstinately to their mother speech, until finally French was banished as an alien tongue. But before this process was accomplished, a multitude of French words had been absorbed into the language, and through the same medium, many more of Scandinavian and Low Latin origin. From these various elements our nomenclature has been built up.

The custom of using surnames began in England after the Norman Conquest. This significant change was not brought about solely by the invasion, for it was a movement that was already spreading through the more populous countries of Europe. The rise of the large towns, and the growing populations in country districts made it increasingly difficult to identify an individual who bore only one name. When as often happened this individual bore a common name like John or Thomas, confusion arose and it had been found convenient to confer a nickname on him. A nickname is originally an eke name, or an additional name *agnomen*, that supplements the information given in the font-name. In this sense all surnames are nicknames.

For centuries before surnames were used to distinguish the individual and the family, nicknames proved a useful makeshift ; and just as Early English kings were known as " the Confessor " and " the Unready " so their subjects were known as " the Brave," " the Strong," " the Fair," or " the Long." But these names were not permanent, and passed away with those that bore them. The practice extended as the need for unmistakable identification became more urgent. But at last pressure of circumstances prevailed and family names began to be adopted so that *William atte Hill* and his descendants became known first as *atte Hill*, and in the course of time simply *Hill*, and *John a Guildford* adopted the family name of *Guildford*.

Philologists have not been able to decide exactly when surnames were first adopted in England. Some maintain that the Saxons were the first to assume them. Searle in the introduction to his *Onomasticon Anglo-Saxonicum* (Cambridge, 1897) says that an attempt was made by Anglo-Saxons to make up for lack of surnames by giving children names in which the themes of the father's names were found, and gives several instances in which this occurred. Amongst others he mentions *Eormenred* of Kent, whose children were called *Eormenbeorh*, *Eormenburh*, and *Eormengyth*.

Canon Taylor, whose views on this subject deserve

consideration, says that in the south, surnames were to be found at the beginning of the twelfth century, and that in the northern counties they were not universal until the end of the fourteenth.

Camden in his *Remaines Concerning Britaine,* expresses his opinion on the subject in his usual downright fashion. " About the yeare of our Lord 1000," he says, " surnames began to be taken up in France. But not in England till about the time of the Conquest, or else a little before, under King Edward the Confessor, who was all Frenchified. And to this time do the Scottish men also refer the antiquity of their surnames, although Buchanan supposed they were not in use in Scotland many years after. Yet in England certain it is that as the better sort, even from the Conquest by little and little took surnames, so they were not setled among the common people fully until about the time of King Edward II, but still used according to the father's name. . . . So it seemed a disgrace for a gentleman to have but one single name, as the meaner sort and bastards had. For the daughter and heir of Fitz Hamon, a great Lard, when King Henry I would have married her to his base son, Robert, she first refusing, answered :

> It were to me a great shame
> To have a Lard withoutin his twa name.

Whereupon the King his father gave him the name of Fitz Roy who after was Earl of Gloucester, and the only worthy of his age in England."

In England the surname was as Sir T. Browne calls it

a " gentilitous appelation," and was assumed only by knights and landowners. Next the merchants and traders took them and finally the peasantry.

But in the north of England, Scotland and Ireland, the inhabitants did not take kindly to the new custom.

In his *Special Report on Surnames in Ireland* issued as a Blue Book in 1894 Sir Robert Matheson quotes a statute of 1366 which provided *inter alia* that English settlers in Ireland were to use only the English language and take English names.

According to the same authority, a law was passed in 1465 (5 Ed. IV, cap. 3) " that every Irishman that dwells betwixt or among English settlers in the County of Dublin, Myeth, *Vriell* and Kildare . . . shall take to him an English surname of one town, as *Sutton, Chester, Trynn, Skryne, Corke, Kinsall;* or colour, as *white, black, brown* ; or arte or science, as smith or carpenter ; or office as cooke, butler."

Here we have plain instructions from the legislators of the fifteenth century, as to the form surnames should take. They suggest local, occupative, and nick-names, but make no mention of patronymics.

In Wales hereditary surnames were not in use even among the gentry until the reign of Henry VIII and were not generally established until a much later period.

The Editor of *Registra Antiqua de Llantillo,* 1577-1644 says that between these dates surnames were just becoming general in Wales.

Even in England the change was only effected by slow degrees. The peasant of the Middle Ages, unlettered and ignorant, who owed his daily bread to

the favour of his overlord, looked with dread and
suspicion on new customs. A freeman only in name,
he fought a daily battle with want, and was often
vanquished and famished in the struggle, and the
absorbing thought of that struggle stifled his ambition
and destroyed his pride. Surnames, or as they were
generally called *sir*names, were for the knights and
gentry who bore heraldic devices on their shields, and
stamped documents with private seals, but not for
him. His cousin in the large town had a happier lot,
and enjoyed a fuller life. His liberties were assured by
Royal Charter and he plied his craft peacefully, secure
in the knowledge that his Guild would protect him
from the wrong doer and marauder. Like his fellows
he welcomed the new custom which facilitated intercourse, and stabilised his position as the head of a
family.

The people in outlying districts still clung to the old
habit of using only baptismal names centuries after
surnames had been adopted in the towns. A record
of the year 1444 shows the easy manner in which
they were changed at that date. From this document we learn that in one family the elder brother
took the local name of *Asheby*. His brother became
Adam Wilson ; and Adam Wilson's son styled himself
John Adkynson.

In Surtees' *Durham*, Vol. 3, a document entitled
De Tribus fratribus bondis de Chilton is quoted, in which
there appear as sons and grandsons of *Ydo Towter*,—
Nicholas Pudding, Richard Marshall or *Diccon Smith,
Jopson*, and *Rogerson*.

In the *Thoresby MSS.* (circa 1704) we read :

" The ancient British way of using the father's and grandfather's christian name instead of the *Nomina Gentilitia* is not yet wholly laid aside in these parts of England (Yorkshire). A pious and ingenious person (my kinsman by marriage) was but the second of his family who had continued the same surname, which had till then been varied as the christian name of the father was, though they were persons of considerable estate. His grandfather Peter, being the son of William, was called *Peter-Williamson ;* his father was called *William Peterson*, which continued till about 1670, when they assumed the surname of *Peters.*

" A friend of mine in Halifax asking the name of a pretty boy that begged relief was answered : ' William a Bills a Toms a Luke.' "

The writer goes on to state that in the surrounding villages the people were still known by the places where they lived. Thus, when he inquired for Henry Cockraft, he could " hear of no such person though he was within two bow-shots of the house." But at length he found him under the name of *Chaumer mon* (chamber man). He then goes on to explain that *chaumer mon* is not to be taken for *camerarius*, but the inhabitant of the chambered house, then a rarity in country villages.

I. Surnames fall into four great classes. The largest of these comprises those taken from places of origin or present address as in *de Leycestre* which represents the modern names *Leicester* and *Lester*, or *ate Hull* for *Hull* or *Hill*. These are known as Local names.

II. The second class includes those derived from a father or ancestor, as in *Wilson*, the son of *Wil* or *Johnson* the son of *John*.

III. Names from the third class are from occupations or office, as in *Smith, Wright, Chandler, Cook*.

IV. The fourth class includes all nicknames. Of these there is an immense variety. Among them are names of birds, beasts, fishes, terms descriptive of personal attributes, as well as oaths and phrase names. Examples of these are *Brown, Wolf, Finch, Pike, Goodspeed*, and *Pardow* (from *pardieu*).

But there are many names that cannot be attributed to any one of the above classes. Some of these may be explained as from two or three different sources. Thus *Martin*, one of the commonest baptismal names used as a surname, is in some cases an animal nickname representing the *marten*. *Lammas* from a place name in Norfolk is also for *Lammas*, loaf mass, one of the feast days of the Church. *March* is a personal name from *Mark ;* it is also a local name from the village *March* in Cambridge. It may also represent a dweller near a *marsh*. *Tibbles* represents *Isabella* as well as *Theobald*. *Myer* and *Myers* are occupative names from *mire* O.Fr. for a doctor. It is also local for *atte mire*. The name *Four* stands for the numeral, and also represents French *four*, an oven.

Few names are susceptible to more explanations of origin than the surname *Bugle*. It is undoubtedly a local name from a small village in the West Country. But it is also a nickname and represents the wild ox (Mid. Engl. *bugle*), and also the musical instrument so dear to the hearts of Boy Scouts. Skeat also explains bugle as from the French *bugle*, a plant. It is also a kind of pad for the hair (Low Latin, *bugoli* pl.).

Gold is a nickname, as well as an Anglo-Saxon personal name. *Nelson* is for the son of *Neil*, but also stands for the son of Nell (Ellen). One of King Arthur's famous knights gives us the surname *Kay*, but we also get it from the more prosaic *quay*, a wharf which in Mid. English was *Key* and *Kaye*.

Badger is an occupative name, and according to Bailey stands for " one that buys corn or other provisions in one place, in order to sell them in another." In other words a pedlar or huckster. But *Badger* is also an animal nickname, and indicates the popular name of the *brock*.

Seymour from *St. Maur* is a local name ; but when representing *seamer*, the tailor, it is occupative. The word seamer has long passed out of use but the feminine forms, *seamstress* and *sempstress*, remain.

Parry has both French and Welsh origins. *Benson* is from *Benjamin* and *Benedict*. *Tait* is an Anglo-Saxon name. It also represents French *Tête*, a head. *Ely* stands for the cathedral city in the Fens ; and also for the prophet *Elias*. *Moss* is a local name. It is also personal, from *Moses*. *Cross* is familiar as a local name, but sometimes it is also a nickname. *Perry* has at least three origins, one local and the others baptismal.

Through coming from diverse sources it is not difficult to understand why several of these names occur so frequently in Directories.

Conversely we find that many simple names appearing in the early records have developed many variations through eccentricities in spelling and dialectical usages. Thus from the Anglo-Saxon Eoforwine we have *Irwin, Erwin, Urwin*, and *Everwin*. For the *grieve's son* there are *Grayson, Grierson* and other variations, found principally in Scotland and the north of England. Of some surnames the variations run to a dozen or more, while even in short and simple names we note such changes as *Smith, Smithyes, Smythe;* and *Brown, Broun* and *Browne*.

As surnames first came into fashion at a relatively late period in history documentary evidence of the earliest examples is abundant. Many of these records are of unimpeachable authority, and the greatest historical value. The most important are :

Domesday Book. William I must have had a kindly thought for the philologists of later centuries, when he caused this record to be prepared in 1086, for it has been a gold mine to investigators, and enabled them to solve many knotty problems that otherwise would have defied solution. It contains the names of thousands of persons, and the places where they lived, written phonetically in Norman French.

The Hundred Rolls compiled two centuries later is a record of a similar kind and equally valuable. It appeared in 1273 when the Angevin Kings ruled the greater part of France as well as England, and French had displaced the Norman dialect as the language of the Court and ruling classes.

In addition to these there are the Pipe Rolls, the

Charter Rolls, the Fine Rolls, the Patent Rolls, Writs of Parliament, the Inquisitiones post mortem, and many minor records, all of which cover a period of about two hundred and fifty years from the middle of the twelfth century.

Thus in the Hundred Rolls we get such entries as Mathew de Cambreye, B. de Calthorpe, Nicholes le Carter, Geoffrey le Cachepol, Hugh de la Chapele, Thombarne (Tom's child), *Wilbarne* (Will's child), G. le *Fittere* (Joiner), Baldwin le *Folle* (Old French *fol*, a fool), John le *Freman*, Roger *Wyseman*, John *Godyf* (modern, *Goodeve*, from Godiva).

These names, except the last, present no difficulty, and after the wear and tear of centuries, show little change. But when in the same records we meet entries such as John *Rattilbagge*, *Wadeinlove* (*Waddilove*), *Plaunterose*, *Bonenfaut* (for *bon enfant*), *Sadelbowe*, *le Toghe* (*Tuff*), *le Swon* (*Swan*), *Cullebene* and *Turnepeny* we recognise the gap that separates us from the Middle Ages. Some of the names in the latter list are now probably obsolete.

The examples given here are in Anglo-French or English. But there are many entries in Latin as *Edric de Ultra Usam* (Pipe Rolls), *Sutor* for shoemaker, Ralph *cum manibus* (*Hands*). Occasionally the Latin form still flourishes side by side with the English name.

If we turn to literature we find surnames treated in careless fashion. In the oldest version of *Chevy Chase*, copied out by Richard Sheale, the names of the leaders who fought in that battle are given as " the perse out off northombarlande," and Douglas whose name in the space of forty lines is indifferently spelt as *dogles*, *doglas*, *duglas*, *dogglas*. How the supporters of these doughty warriors fared we learn in the following lines :

> " thear was slayne withe the lard perse, *ser John* of *agerstone ;*
> Ser Rogar the hinde *hartly, ser* William the bolde *hearone ;*
> Ser *Jorg* the worthe *loumle*, a knyghte of great Renowen ;
> Ser Raff the *Ryche* Rugbe, with dyntes wear beaten dowene ;
> for Wetharryngton my harte was wo, that ever he slayne shulde be ;
> for when both his leggis wear hewyne in to, yet he knyled and fought on his kny.
> ther was slayne, with the dougheti duglas, ser *herve* the *monggombyrry ;*
> Sir *dauy lwdale*, that worthe was, his sister's son was he ;
> Sir *charls a murry* in that place, that neuer a foot wolde fle ;
> *sir hewe maxwelle*, a larde he was, with the doglas dyd he dey."

In the later version of the poem *Monggombyrry* is given as *Mountgomerye*, of which the modern form is *Montgomery*. Sir Walter Scott explains *Agerstone* or *Haggerston* as of *Edgerston* between Jedburgh and the Cheviots. Skeat questions this and suggests that *Agerstone* is from a place called Haggerston close to Holy Island and adds that two *Akerstons* are mentioned in the Ballad of Bosworth Feilde, Percy Folio MS.

Sir Roger the hinde, *hartly*. Here *the hinde* means the courteous or gentle, while *hartly* (Hartley) is a local name. *Hearone* is a nickname and stands for Heron ; *loumle* is for *Lumley*. Skeat points out that " my Lord Lumley " is mentioned in both the " Ballad of Scotish Feilde," and the " Ballad of Bosworth Feilde."

In the later version of " Chevy Chase " *Rugbe* is given as *Rebby*.

Wetharryngton, later *Witherington*, is a local name from *Widrington*, a place north of Morpeth in Northumberland. *Sir dauy lwdale* is Sir David *Lambwell* in the later version of the poem ; while *sir charls* a (of) *Murry* is according to the same authority Sir Charles *Morrell*. *Maxwell* is self explanatory.

But the scanty literature of the Middle Ages does not help us much in discovering the sources of surnames. It enables us to understand the significance of many words from which surnames were formed, and illustrates their modifications and developments. In *Cocke Lorrelle* there is a long and almost bewildering list of traders and craftsmen, about some of whom Langland writes more vividly in his *Vision of Piers Plowman :*

> Baronns and Burgeis
> and Bondemen also . . .
> Bakers, bochers
> and breusters monye ;
> Masons, menours,
> and mony other craftes,
> Dykers and delvers,
> That don heare dedes ille . . .
> Cookes and heore knaves
> Cryen " Hote pies hote !
> Goode gees and grys !
> Go we, dyne, gon we ! "

" Go we " was a common exclamation and means " Come along." These old writings are of absorbing interest to the philologist and student of literature, but those who would learn something of surnames will use their time to more advantage if they study the records already mentioned and try to find the equivalents of the names entered in them in modern directories. Here there is immense wealth of material, and much that has never attracted the attention of the investigator. In the books of ancient churches, and the archives of some of our oldest towns, many documents lie hidden that some day will bring joy to the hearts of those that discover them.

Despite transport facilities and the cheapness and quickness of modern travel there are tens of thousands of families still dwelling in the shires in which their family trees were first rooted. In the Cumberland and Westmoreland dales are many farmers whose families have tilled the same lands for hundreds of years, and there is no reason to doubt that the same applies to every other part of Great Britain.

As Mr. Hy. B. Guppy has shown in his interesting book, *Homes of Family Names in Great Britain* (1890), there are surnames that have never spread beyond the boundaries of two or three counties. Others are well-known only in five or six.

Among the names well represented in from twenty to thirty counties of England are Adams, Andrews, Bailey, Baker, Bennett, Brooks, Carter, Chapman, Cole, Cooper, Davis, Edwards, Ellis, Foster, Harrison, Hill, *Hunt*, Jackson, James, King, Lee, Mason, Matthews, Mitchell, Moore, Morris, Palmer, Parker, Phillips, Reid, Richardson, Roberts, Rogers, Sanders, Shepherd, Stephens, Thompson, Walker, Ward, Watson, Webb, Williams, Wood, Young.

A few are to be found in the Directories of every

county. Taken in alphabetical order these are :
Allen, Brown, Clark, Cook, Green, Hall, Harris,
Johnson, Jones, Martin, Robinson, Smith, Taylor,
Turner, White, Wilson and Wright.

It is scarcely necessary to remark that the most
popular of these names is that of Smith. In the
British Islands, with the possible exception of Wales,
in most countries of Europe, and in the United States
of America, the Smiths or their foreign representatives
far outnumber those of any other family.

In a return prepared at Edinburgh in 1899 showing the
proportion of Smiths to the bearers of other names in
Glasgow, Edinburgh, Inverness and Perth the following
figures are given :

In Glasgow one in every 130 inhabitants is a
Campbell ; one in 129 is *Wilson ;* one in 128, *Robertson ;* one in 125, *Miller ;* one in 124, *Thomson ;* one
in 121, *Brown ;* and one in every 88 bears the name of
Smith.

In Edinburgh the proportions of *Smiths* was even
higher, one in fifty. While *Brown, Robertson* and
Stewart were one in fifty-nine, one in sixty-two, and
one in ninety-eight respectively.

In Inverness and Perth, the name *Smith* loses pride
of place. In the former town one in every thirty-three
is a *Frazer ;* one in forty-three is called *Macdonald ;*
and *Mackenzie* is represented by one in forty-eight,
Smith is a bad fourth with one in 270.

In Perth, *Smith* comes third, the first and second
places being taken by *Stewart* and *Young.*

But though the name *Smith* appears more frequently

in Directories than any other it is evenly distributed and does not cause confusion through an overwhelming preponderance in one province or district, as occurs in some parts of Scotland and Wales. We have seen in the return just given that in Inverness one person in thirty-three is named *Frazer*, and one in forty-three *Macdonald*, but in some Welsh towns the proportion of *Jonses* is much greater, so great indeed that the name forms a perfect disguise. There are parishes in Scotland where the majority of the inhabitants answer to the same surname.

This breakdown of the surnominal system is amusingly illustrated in an article in *Blackwood's Magazine* (March, 1842), to which Sir Herbert Maxwell drew attention in *Notes and Queries*, May 22nd, 1915.

From this it appears there were in the tiny seaport of Buckie, twenty-five males who possessed the name of George Cowie. To distinguish these from each other, they were given nicknames, and were readily identified by their neighbours by such names as Carrot, Doodle, Neep, Big-lugs, Bam, Hilldom, Collop, Stoattie, Snuffers, Rochie, Toothie and Todlowrie.

A story is also told of a stranger who sought out a fisherman named Alexander White but did not know either his nickname or house. He asked a girl :

" Could you tell me fa'r (where) Sammy Fite lives ? "

" Filk (which) Sammy Fite ? "

" Muckle (Big) Sammy Fite."

" Filk muckle Sammy Fite ? "

" Muckle lang Sammy Fite."

" Filk muckle lang Sammy Fite ? "

" Muckle lang gleyed (squinting) Sammy Fite."

" Oh ! Its Goup-the lift (Stare at the Sky) ye're seeking," said the girl, " and fat the deevil for dinna ye speer (inquire) for the man by his richt name at ance."

In still more recent times the confusion caused through the popularity of some surnames has been overcome in some parts of Scotland by adding his wife's maiden name to a married man's surname, e.g. James Frazer (Logie), James Frazer (Katis).

Even in England where surnames are more numerous and more evenly distributed the same confusion sometimes arises.   In the Foreword to his *Dictionary of Surnames*, Mr. Harrison quotes an account from the *Southport Guardian* of December 3rd, 1913, of a supper to fishermen which was attended by thirty-one people with the surname *Wright*, all of whom were known to their neighbours by picturesque and more or less complimentary nicknames.

How are we to account for the extraordinary pre-eminence of the name *Smith*?   A slight knowledge of industrial life in the Middle Ages makes this easy to understand.

The smith or hammer worker follows an occupation that is as old as Tubal Cain.   His craft was one of the few that were indispensable in primitive times.   It was exercised everywhere.   Wherever a settlement was formed, however small it might be, there were found the smith and his forge.   In days before some branches of the craft became specialised, his rough skill was put to a hundred uses.   He made the plough and other agricultural implements; he shod the horses; fashioned the metal collar of the serf; made the bill spear and breastplate. Some of the compounds among our surnames serve to remind us that he was a maker of many kinds of ironmongery. Thus we have *Redsmith, Shoesmith, Shearsmith, Scasmith* (Scythe-smith from A. S. *Sigthe*, a scythe), *Naysmith* (Knife-smith), and *Brownsmith*. But the name is derived from other sources as well. It is also local and indicates that one of its original owners lived at the *smeeth* or smooth field. In some cases it is also a nickname, and represents the *smeed*, a small diving bird, which was also called the *smee* and *smeeth*.

But the name is principally one of occupation, and the number of *Smiths* of local and nickname origin must be relatively rare. Otherwise how are we to account for the popularity of the name in other countries?

Fearon, the French equivalent for *Smith* (from Old French *feron*), a smith, is also well represented in modern Directories.

From the foregoing we have seen that English surnames like the words of our common speech, have come to us from many sources. Many Saxon and Norse names which were in common use as font-names in the eleventh century still survive as surnames, but they were overshadowed by those introduced by the Normans, and have since remained in a state of suspended animation and formed few or no derivatives. Through Old French and the Norman dialect we inherited a large number of Old German and Scandinavian

names, and by way of the same media many more
from Low Latin. To these were added a considerable
number, introduced by the Celtic peoples of Northern
Scotland, Wales, and Ireland. When to these we join
the many names brought in by the immigrants who
flocked to these shores for centuries in an unending
stream, names that were strangely twisted into an
Anglicised form by the English officials who recorded
them, we cease to wonder at the strange hotch-potch
of words that fill up our Directories, and marvel that
among them there are so few names apparently of
foreign origin.

In the reign of Queen Elizabeth and afterwards under
the Stuarts many thousands of Huguenots, harried and
persecuted by successive French Kings, sought asylum
in England. This movement reached its culminating
point when in 1685 the Edict of Nantes was revoked,
and the last of the French Protestants were banished
from their native land. So considerable was this
inflow of refugees, that the English rulers who eagerly
welcomed them, allotted an annual sum of £200,000
for their comfort and support. A few years earlier
(in 1675) Charles II allowed the French refugees to
meet in the little chapel of the Savoy, and the Church
still enjoys by direct inheritance the grant in perpetuity
made to it by the merry monarch.

These immigrants settled in all parts of the United
Kingdom but the majority took up their residence in
London, principally in Spitalfields, St. Giles and Soho.
They were of all classes, and among them were men
who by inventive genius, force of character and wealth

had occupied positions of great authority in their native land. Among them were some of the founders of the Bank of England.

These retained their names unchanged, and include many that have added lustre to our annals. But the majority were of the humbler sort and included artisans and workers in crafts, which until then had been strange to England. These people, received by the native workers with the suspicion and distrust always accorded to foreigners, were only too eager to hide their identity, and either took English names on their own initiative, or had their names anglicised for them by parish officials, innocent of all philological knowledge.

It may be noted incidentally that the French term *huguenot* is from the personal name *Huguenot*. This is a diminutive of the French *Hugon*, accusative case from the nominative *Hugues*, Hugh, which in its turn is from German *eidgenoss*, a sworn ally. From this it became in popular usage *eiugenot*, *higueno* to indicate a Protestant. The term *Huguenot* was, according to Skeat, in use two centuries at least before the Reformation.

The Huguenots were the last of the persecuted peoples who came, in considerable numbers, to seek asylum in this country. Though there has since been a constant stream of immigrants there has been no incursion on any considerable scale.

Generally speaking the people who took up their homes in this country were of a better class than those who migrate only for their own advantage. Mostly

they were Flemings, German and Swiss Protestants
fleeing from religious persecution, or political refugees
seeking freedom from oppression.   In addition to these
were the builders, skilled craftsmen and artists brought
from Holland, Italy and Spain by Henry VIII and
later monarchs.   There were, needless to say, many
among these immigrants whose departure from their
native land must have been witnessed by their compatriots with relief.   But after making full allowance for undesirables, these immigrants exercised a
beneficent influence on the fortunes of England and
helped to make it for a time the workshop of the
world.

Many names borne by these immigrants of the
by-gone centuries have been made illustrious by
descendants who have won renown in many walks of
life.   Of these some examples will be given in a later
chapter.

Spelling and Pronunciation

One of the chief difficulties confronting the student
when comparing the names of the ancient Rolls with
those of the modern Directory is the difference of form
and spelling.   Great changes have taken place in
pronunciation since early times, and as Mr. A. J. Ellis
pointed out in his exhaustive study of the subject,
some of the most remarkable of these changes took
place during the civil wars of the fifteenth century and
the latter part of the seventeenth and former part of
the eighteenth centuries.   Even the speech and accent
of the early years of the last century differ much from

our own. Mr. G. W. E. Russell tells us in his *Collections and Recollections* that Lord John Russell, like other high-bred people of his time, talked of " cowcumbers " and " laylocks " called a woman a " 'ooman," and was " much obleeged " where a more degenerate age is content to be obliged. In less august circles the change is equally great, and the Sam Wellers of our own time—if there are any—no longer speak of " vidders " and " wittles."

There can be little doubt as Mr. Ellis maintains that much of the gross confusion in modern English spelling is due to these great changes in pronunciation. As Professor Skeat caustically remarks, " our modern spelling exhibits no principle at all, but merely illustrates the inconvenience of separating symbols from sounds."

" In England there is no controlling authority, like the French Academy to regulate spelling, or give guidance as to pronunciation. When reform comes, it is rarely, deliberately planned, and just happens. So it has been with spelling. For good or ill, the printers to suit their own convenience and according to a system—or want of system—of their own, made spelling uniform, and as the reading public raised no serious objection to this revised spelling, it became standardised."

The spelling of old English was not uniform. But much of it was better than our modern spelling, for it was at least phonetic. Every writer, according to his knowledge, endeavoured by the symbols he used to represent the sounds of words. As there were then many dialects so the pronunciation of words varied and therefore the spelling.

But though the spelling of the language has been made uniform, no attempt has been made to normalise the spelling of names. Such a task was beyond the power of the printers, for of the many generations of people who have lived and died in England only an infinitesimally small proportion has ever had their names recorded in print. " The short and simple annals of the poor," were limited to entries of birth, marriage and death, and as prior to the nineteenth century most of these people had not the vaguest idea as to how their names were spelt this task was left to the discretion of parish officials. Even educated people three centuries ago spelt their names as fancy dictated, and from the varied spellings of the names of Shakespeare, Raleigh, and other famous men of the sixteenth and seventeenth centuries, we find that uniformity in spelling names was not regarded as of any importance.

The following varied spellings of the name *Raleigh* are given in the Index to Reg. Univ., Oxford : *Ralegh, Raleighe, Rallegh, Raughley, Raughlie, Raughly, Raugleigh, Rauleigh, Rauly, Rawlie, Rawleigh, Rawley, Rawleygh, Rawlei, Rawlighe, Rawlye, Raylye.*

Government and municipal officials were equally indifferent. Thus in the Bristol Records, 1654-1685, we find the name Bristol spelt *Bristow, Bristol, Bristoll,* while in many other names there are similar variations. But the most amazing instance is that given by Canon Bardsley in reference to the name Blenkinsop :

" On April 23rd, 1470, Elizabeth *Blynkkynesoppe* of

Blynkkynsoppe, widow of Thomas *Blynkyensope* of *Blynkkensope* received a general pardon." In this sentence of eighteen words the name is spelt in four different ways.

From this orthographic independence of our ancestors arises that variety in modern surnames which sometimes amuses but always interests us. Thus we have the variants *Adkin*, *Adkins*, *Atkins*, *Atkinson* and *Adkinson* from *Adam*. From *Borough* we get the variants *Bury*, *Borrow*, *Berry* and *Brough*. From *Guinever* of Arthurian legend *Genever*, *Gillever*, *Jennifer* are derived. We have three surnames, *Hearne*, *Herne* and *Hurne* from M. E., *herne*, a " corner," and from read (red), *Read*, *Reid* and *Reed*.

Many names are so altered in form by careless usage through hundreds of years that it is impossible to conjecture their origins. The derivations of others seem so improbable, that it is only by comparison with similar forms in other languages that we can settle our doubts as to their origin.

But though some names obstinately refuse to yield up their secrets, and others confront us with difficult problems, the most amazing feature of the old records is that a great number of the surnames inscribed in them are almost identical in form with their modern representatives. Let us take an example or two from the hundreds that could be given. In the Hundred Rolls we find *Hervey le Palmer ;* and *Geoffrey le Palmer* in the Calendarium Inquisitorium Post Mortem. Again in the Writs of Parliament the name of Walter *le* Pardoner is inscribed. The callings of the palmer and the pardoner passed away with the Middle Ages. But the names that stood for these callings remain, and except that the definite article preceding the surnames has been deleted, they are unchanged. The callings of the *Somenur*, *le Bedel*, *le Almoner*, and *Bedeman* have long vanished, but these surnames of the early rolls still survive in *Sumner*, *Beadell*, *Aumonier*, *Badman* and *Bidman*.

Again in the Hundred Rolls the name *Gris* appears, meaning *pig*. It is also inscribed in the Writs of Parliament as *Grise*. The name is still a common one in Cumberland as *Grice*, as are its compounds *Grise-wood* and *Grisdale*. Other names from the same record are Richard *le Bere*, of which *Bear* is the modern representative ; Elina *le Wolfe* which survives in *Wolf*, *Wolff*, *Wolffe* and other derivatives. The names *Fox*, *Beaver* and *Squirrel* are still with us. The early scribes entered them as *le Fox*, *le Bever*, and *le Squirrel*.

Another point that impresses even the most casual student of surnames is their extraordinary diversity. Our forefathers borrowed them from every possible source. No object was too insignificant and none too great, for its name to be used for this purpose. In the old lists we find names of tiny field flowers as well as those of countries and even continents. The points of the compass furnished their quota of names, and those of animals, birds and fishes were also pressed into service. The mountain, the stream, the wood, and the dale, as well as every feature of the countryside, all served the purposes of nomenclature. The names of towns, villages and estates, as well as their notable features, the wells, crosses, manor houses, monasteries, shop signs, were also used. To these must be added the great army of surnames from baptismal names, Bible names, craft and trade names, and even some derived from oaths, exclamations and phrases. As if these were not enough we have also official names, pageant names, others from costume, colour, kinship, physical nicknames, musical instruments, implements and wares of all kind. To these must be added a considerable number of foreign names.

Of these a general survey will be given in the following chapters.

CHAPTER II

LOCAL NAMES

> For words, like Nature, half reveal and half conceal
> the soul within.—TENNYSON.

A DANISH monarch made England a nation. Norman
William added a new strain to the Saxon blood-stream,
and called into being the English people.

But before this was achieved, many adjustments
were to be made. A large and constantly growing
population had to be settled in the new land. The
stern edicts of Feudalism were enacted. The Norman
barons were established in town and country, side by
side with the clergy who received a large share of the
spoil, and with a business-like promptitude and care, for
which historians owe him thanks, William I set out the
results of these transactions in that famous document
that we know as *Domesday Book*.

Despite differences of language, habits and culture
victors and vanquished quickly settled down together.
In less than two centuries the distinction between
Norman and Saxon had disappeared, and only Englishmen remained, who spoke dialects of a tongue that was
in time to become the common speech of hundreds of
millions.

The Norman conquest bridged the narrow seas
and made England a continental people. Trade

followed the Conqueror's banners, and from an insular state, England became a nation with interests in all parts of Europe. In the century that followed William's victory at Senlac, hosts of Norman and Angevin traders voyaged to England and bartered strange wares for native produce. Many settled in the growing towns and the populations of these rapidly increased. London became a hive of industry and towns like Boston (Lincolnshire), Norwich, York, Winchester, and Bristol rose to importance and influence. The iron discipline of the Feudal system hastened the growth of these larger communities, and made them harbours of refuge for the oppressed, as well as checks on the power of the nobles.

In these larger towns differences of language must for many years have hampered intercourse between the different sections of the inhabitants ; for to the native the speech of Norman or Frenchman was only a shade more incomprehensible than other dialects of his own language.

Added to this was the constantly increasing difficulty of personal identifications, due to the sole use of baptismal names. This difficulty was at last overcome by the adoption of surnames as has already been explained in the Introductory Chapter.

Let us consider those that were first adopted.

The largest class of surnames is those derived from places. They were also the first to become hereditary. These Local names are all-embracing in their scope and cover practically every ancient British place name in the Gazetteer as well as hundreds of French, Flemish and other continental places and estates. They also include names of countries as well as provinces, counties, towns, villages.

Among the first to adopt these local surnames were the fighting men who carved their way to fortune at Hastings, and received as reward for their services grants of English estates. Camden, shrewdest and quaintest of the older etymologists, declares " neither is there any village in Normandy that gives not denomination to some family in England." But the sources of English surnames are not confined by the borders of the old Duchy. They came from all parts of France and Flanders, from the shores of the Mediterranean, and the thriving sea-ports of the Baltic.

We find among these in old records the proud and swelling names *de Granville*, *Villiers*, *Mortimer*, *Mowbray*, *Percy* and *Pierpont*. The old chroniclers gloried in the sound of these names, and recited many interesting stories to account for their origin. But etymologists shake their heads over these legends and in prosaic terms explain that *Grenville* and *Granville* are French place names ; that *Mortimer* comes from one of the two *Morte-mers* in France, while the *Mowbrays* take their name from the village Montbrai. Those who bear the name *Villiers* will feel no surprise that their name is so prevalent, when they learn that there are more than fifty villages in France of this name, from any or all of which migrants may have come to England. The name *Percy*, immortalised in English story by Shakespeare comes from one of three obscure French villages that bear the same name.

From the Chapelries of Normandy we get many surnames that still wax and flourish. Thus *Sellinger* is from St. Ledger. *Somers* is from St. Omer. It also comes from Summers. *Semper* is from St. Pierre, as is *Simper;* *Sillery* is from St. Hillary; *Seymour* from St. Maur. But *Seymour* like *Somers* originates from more than one source, and some of them were *Seamers* (tailors). We derive the names *Senley* and *Sanley* from St. Liz. *Samand* and *Sandeman* are modern forms of St. Amand, though *Sandeman* may also as Bardsley suggests mean Sander's man, or the servant of Alexander. Another source is, as Mr. Weekley suggests in *The Romance of Names* (page 64) the Mid. English word *Sandeman*, a messenger. *Sidney* is from St. Denys ; *Sinclair* and *Sinkler* from St. Clair ; whilst from St. Paul we get several surnames, e.g. *Simpole, Semphill, Sample,* and *Semple*.

In old records we find the names of many immigrants from the Low Countries. Thus in the Rolls of Parliament there are entries like *Ascelyn le Fleming,* and *Baldwin le Fleming,* the forerunners of the present day *Flemings*. Other settlers acquired surnames in the same way, as Dench (Danish), *France, French, Norman* and *Welsh* with its variants *Welch, Walsh,* and *Wallis*.

Brittany, in its French form *Bretagne* is responsible for a number of surnames—*Britten, Brett* and *Brittain*.

Maine, Mansell and *Mayne* are from the Duchy of Maine, though *Mayne* like *Main* is also from *Maynard*. From Anjou we have *Angers* and *Angwin*, while from the province of Burgundy we have *Burgon*, *Burgin*, *Burgoine*. Gascony furnishes the surnames *Gascoigne*, *Gascoin*, *Gascoine*, *Gascoyne* and *Gaskin*.

From Picardy we have *Pycard*, *Pickard* and *Power* (Early English *Poeir*, Old Fr. *Pohier*, a Pickard).

Poitou. There are many variants from *Poitevin* (a native of Poitou). In the Hundred Rolls the name appears as *Potewyne*. Modern names from it are *Poidevin*, *Portwine* and *Potwin*. Lorraine is the source of *Loring* and *Lorraine*. Our modern *Espino* and *Spain* have their old-time counterparts in *de Spaigne* and *de Espagne*.

In his tale of Sir Thopas, Chaucer mentions that coin of the Genoese republic known as the *Jane*.

> His robe was of ciclatoun
> That cost many a *jane*.

Jane, Old Fr. Jaune, *Genoa*. From this term we get the surnames *Jayne*, *Janeway* and *Jannaway*.

The insular prejudice of English people against foreigners was much stronger in the Middle Ages than now, and it must be admitted that they had good grounds for this dislike. The Normans had seized their lands and despoiled them of their property. The foreigner administered justice and State affairs, and the native owed allegiance to Norman baron and French Abbot.

But one class at least of the strangers from overseas won the esteem and confidence of English people—the *Easterling*. The merchants, who were so designated came from the shores of the Baltic, and quickly earned a reputation for honesty by the straightforwardness of their dealings. A favourite device of the trade tricksters of the period was that of paying accounts with clipped money, and by so doing acquiring goods at less than market value. Through the dishonest practice of coin-clipping, money lost its standard value, and there was in consequence much wrangling over business transactions. The *Easterling* resorted to none of these tricks. He paid for his purchases in money, that was always full weight, and so was warmly welcomed by the traders he visited. As news of his business dealings spread abroad it became the custom of merchants to demand *Easterling* money for their wares. In time the aphetic form *sterling* was substituted for *Easterling*, so that now the word not only stands as a surname for the successors of these honest traders, but is also a commercial term used in such phrases as " pounds sterling," " sterling value," and " sterling character."

In expressing his tolerance for foreign languages the poet Skelton says :

With *Douch*, with *Spanysh*, my tung can agree.

Douch was the early English equivalent for Dutch, and was applied indiscriminately to foreigners. The old name is still upheld by our *Douch* and *Dowches*.

The French word *Allemand* was also a name given to the stranger from overseas, and occurs in various forms in old records, e.g. *d'Almaine, de Almania*. From these we get the surnames *Allman, Almaine, Dalmain*. In Dalmain the preposition has been joined to the noun.

Most of the counties have made their contribution to the general stock of family names, among them Wiltshire, Cornwall, Kent, Lancashire, Derbyshire, Berkshire, Westmoreland, Cumberland, and Norfolk. Thus in old charters we find Richard *Wilteshire*, Geoffrey *de Cornwalys*, William *de Kent*, Thomas *Derbyshyre*, Adam *de Kent*, and Robert *de Northfolk*. These have come down to us with only some slight modifications in spelling, though we have *Cant* as well as *Kent* for Kent, and the dialectical form *Lankshear* as well as *Lancashire* for the name of the County Palatine. From *Wiltshire* we have both *Wiltshire* and *Willsher*.

SURNAMES FROM TOWNS AND VILLAGES

These are names of origin, and were conferred on those who migrated to a new home. The stranger within the gate was in those days closely questioned as to his business and bluntly asked where he came from. Thus when Peter of Walsham migrated to Norwich he would soon be known to his new acquaintances as *Peter of Walsham*. In course of time the preposition dropped out of the name, and the newcomer was known as Peter *Walsham*. Chronicles of the Middle Ages offer us items of news that contain names of this class. Thus in one we read that in 1342 Sir Robert de Redware robbed a merchant convoy near Lichfield, and that the traders whose goods had been pillaged petitioned their lord the Earl of Arundel beseeching him to obtain redress for them. We discover such names as *Richard de Kellowe* (Bishop of Durham) ; of *Reginald de Rosels*, who allowed the

Abbot of Whitby to build a bridge over the Esk ; of the gorgeous state in which the Bishop of Hereford, *Richard de Swinfield*, travelled, having in his train the clerks of his chapel as well as carters, porters, falconers, grooms and messengers. Also his champion, *Thomas de Bruges*, whose duty it was to fight in the prelate's name, on the occasion of any lawsuit that might end in trial by combat.

In the list of surnames from places of origin the names of the larger towns and cities do not figure so often as those of smaller ones, for the good reason that the general movement was from the village to the town, and from the smaller towns to London, Norwich and Bristol.

In *The Pastons and their England*, from which some of these materials have been gathered there is an extract from a legal document of the fourteenth century taken from the Guildhall archives, that runs as follows " The jurors say that at the hour of Vespers the said William struck with his hand a certain *Johanna de Lillebourne* . . . for opprobrious words that had arisen between them. That seeing this a certain *John Walsham*, a taylor, being moved with anger on her account drew his knife . . . and therewith mortally struck the said William so that he there fell and immediately died. Being asked who were present when this happened the jurors say, the aforesaid William John and Johanna, and a certain *Adam le Irishe* came up and raised the cry . . . Being asked what became of the said John, the jurors say he fled to the church of S. Edmund the King in Langbourne Ward."

Of the three surnames given in this report that of the lady is possibly obsolete. The other two are local and still flourish as *Walsham* and *Irish*.

The names given in the following list, though apparently long represent a very small proportion of the number of names derived from towns and villages. The total number, if extracted from Parish registers and local directories and verified would fill a volume of bulky dimensions.

Among these names are *Aston*, *Acton*, *Derby*, *Bristow* (Bristol), *Kendal*, *Charlton*, *Clifton*, *Cowley*, *Durnford*, *Durham*, *Harley*, *Hereford*, *Mayston* for Maidstone, *Knabwell*, *Lascelles*, *London*, *Manchester*, *Neville*, *Snaith* and *Keyhoe* (Kew, Surrey), and *Kew*. There are many townships that bear the names of *Sutton*, *Kirby*, *Preston* and *Bradford*, and they give useful service as surnames.

Then there are *Birmingham*, *Bedford*, *Bath*, *Boston*, *Bakewell*, *Berwick*, *Beddington*, *Beckenham*, *Chesterton*, *Chesterfield*, *Chichester*, *Colchester*, and *Daintry* and *Daintree* that express phonetically the local name of Daventry. Other popular names are *Deal* and *Deale* from Deal, *Dover*, *Farnham*, *Goring*, *Harrow*, *Hastings*, *Hatfield*, *Keighley* and *Keeley* for Keighley, *Kensington*, *Lincoln*, *Mansfield*, *Pomfret* and *Pomfrett* from Pontefract, *Portsmouth*, *Romney*, *Rye*, *Sheen*, *Salisbury*, *Sherwood*, *Shields*, *Shrewsbury*, *Stafford*, *Stamford*, *Trent*, *Thame*, *Weston*, *Whitby*, *Wimbourne*, *Winchester*, *Windsor*, *Witham*, *Wansborough*, and *Wellington*.

As with every other class of surname many of these names have been changed almost beyond recognition by dialectical usage, and through the eccentric spelling of Norman scribes and the parish clerks who succeeded them.

We have already seen that, following the Conquest, a constant stream of traders flocked to England, and we find evidence of this in the large number of names derived from the provinces, towns, villages and estates of France. Of the names derived from continental cities one of the most interesting is that of *Paris*, on which the greatest of the monastic historians shed the lustre of his genius.

The name of *Lubbock* indicates that those who originally bore the surname hailed from Lübeck. The late Sir John Lubbock, afterwards Lord Avebury, wrote several books that were popular in the eighties and nineties of the last century, but he will in future years be chiefly remembered as the legislator who brought in the Bank Holiday Bill.

Greater than these was that scholar of noble birth, Lanfranc of Pavia, who founded the school at Bec, and was brought to England by the Conqueror and made Archbishop of Canterbury.

But for the most part these names of foreign origin are not of interest, except to those who wish to know why a seaport on the Baltic shores or a chapelry in Anjou should give its name to an English family ; or to the philologist who seeks to extract from a name the truth that lies behind the letters which compose it. Like the gentleman in Molière's play who discovered he had been speaking prose all his life without knowing it, there are staid English citizens who have never guessed that the origin of the names of which they are so proud must be sought on the other side of the English Channel. Yet we find that *Raynes* is derived from Rennes, and *Roan* from Rouen. *Aris* is from Arras, *Bloss* from Blois, while *Callis*, *Callison* and *Challis* have their origin in Calais. *Druce* is from Drena, and *Turney* from Tournay. *Stamp* which has a good English ring and is suggestive of commerce, originates in Étampes. *Leyden* from Leyden, and *Antioch* (Robert de Antiochus) have come down to us unchanged, and need no explanation. *Devereux* originates in d'Évreux, and *Daubeney* from D'Aubigné, while from Bruges we get the anglicised *Bridges* as well as *Bruges*. Chaucer's version of the name was *Brugges* for he says of Sir Thopas :

> Of Brugges were his hosen broun

Cane, *Caine* and *Cain* we may assume to be all from Caen, as it is improbable that any self-respecting family would assume or retain the name of the fratricide, who in all ages has been regarded as a monster of iniquity.

Cullen comes from Cologne, and from Colville spring the names *Colvil*, *Colvile*, *Colvill*, and *Colville*. The surname Florence (John de Florence) needs no explanation. *Gant*, *Gantes*, and *Gaunt* are from Gand (Ghent), and Simon de *Gaunt*, whose name figures in the Hundred Rolls, and who was probably a Flemish wool-dealer, took his name from the same city as "time-honoured Lancaster."

Bullen and *Boleyn* are popular versions of Boulogne.

OTHER SURNAMES OF ORIGIN

Readers have observed from the examples given that it was the fashion, when surnames were first adopted to indicate the place of origin by putting a preposition between the two names. So that newcomers from Rye or Winchester were known as Thomas *a Rye* or William of Winchester.

French prepositions, principally *de*, were also freely employed, not only for names of French origin but also in native ones as well as in *Giles de Debenham* or *Geoffrey de Sutton*. Names like these not only served the purpose of distinguishing their owners from other people, but were passports that challenged investigation. In an age when a man had cause to be suspicious of his neighbour, any information about the stranger within the gate, if only his place of origin, helped to establish good relations. It is easy then to understand that people like *Peter le Newe*, *Walter le Neweman* or *Roger le Straunge*, the forerunners of our *News*, *Newmans* and *Stranges*, were regarded with distrust, as being persons of whom nothing was known. It is a tribute to the strong adhesive properties of nicknames that these *Newes* and *Stranges*, who obviously owed these designations to the good offices of their acquaintances, realised that it would be futile to try and assume any others. So that now, many centuries after their names were first recorded, they still figure as strangers and newmen in our midst.

When the place of origin was not precisely known, or the newcomer came from some village too insignificant to be remembered, geographical terms were employed and he was referred to vaguely as from the north, south or west.   Thus we find in old records entries like *Geoffrey le Northern*, and *de North*, *Thomas le Southern*, *Richard le Westreys*, and in Directories their modern counterparts in *North*, *Northey*, *South*, *Sothern*, *Sotheran*, *West*, *Westray* and *Western*.

CHAPTER III

ADDRESS SURNAMES

WE have considered the class of surnames conferred on the newcomer to town and village, and will now turn to those given to the natives. For these also fall into a separate category and may be described as Address Surnames. These are much more definite in the information they convey.

Instead of telling us vaguely where a man came from these surnames give precise information, as in *John atte Mor, Richard ate Grene, Wat at the Well, William de la Lea* (Hundred Rolls), *John atte Knolle, Robert de Greenslade*. In old records there are many examples of names in these forms.

In *The Pastons and their England* an affidavit by the rector of the church at Winchelsea is quoted wherein he " complaineth of Robert Arnold, *Roger at Gate*, and John Hermit, that on Sunday . . . they came to the church, with force and arms, and against the peace of our Lord the King, to wit, with swords, buckers, daggers, etc., and there in the said chapel . . . they assaulted him, and beat him and wounded him."

In the same book is mentioned another complaint from the Rolls of Parliament in which it is stated by *Agnes atte Wood* that she and her son were beaten and robbed.

In these address surnames the reader will notice that they are attached to the font names by a variety of prepositional forms in English, French and Latin In his *English Surnames*, Canon Bardsley quotes the following variations on the name " Lane " :

Cecilia in the Lane.

Emma a la Lane.

John de la Lane.

John de Lane.

Mariota en le Lane.

Phillipa ate Lane.

Thomas super Lane.

At first names were joined in these different ways, in records as well as in speech, the Normans using the French and Latin and the Saxons the English forms.

Names of this kind are multitudinous, and almost bewildering in their variety. There is scarcely a feature of the countryside or of the little townships of Medieval times that is not represented among them. Natural objects like rivers, hills, dales, meadows, fields, trees, flowers, brooks and fords ; buildings and their parts, crosses, gates, thorpes, burys and towns, all were laid under contribution for purposes of nomenclature.

Names similar to these just mentioned which we find in old rolls and charters recall a social and political organisation different from our own. The Manor house and the Church were then the centres of the community, and around them were dotted the cottages and huts of their dependents. These were distinguished by names like *Atte-broc* (*Brook*), *Thomas atte-More*

(*Moor*), *Nicholas de Apelyerd* (*Appleyard*), *Adam de Ashurst*, *John ate-felde* (*Field* and *Atfield*), *Roger atten Ashe, John de Ashlegh, William atte Bee, Robert de la Beche* (*Beech*), *Stephen atte Brigende*, *Robert de Broadhaye* (*Broadhay*), *Robert atte Chirchyate* (*Churchgate*), *John atte Churchestighele* (*Churchstile*), *Peter ate Ford* (*Ford*), *Robert atte Gore* (*Gore*), *Antony de Greneslade* (*Greenslade*), *John at Hil* (*Hill*), *John de la How* (*Howe*), *Ralph de la Leye* (*Lea*), *William atte Noke* (*Nokes*), *William Rowentree* (*Rowntree*), *John de la Sale* (*Sale*), *Richard ate Spitels* (*Spittal*), *John de la Stone* (*Stone*), and *William atte Strete* (*Street*). The first of these names *Broke*, now *Brook*, *Brooke*, like several of the others needs no elucidation. It is well represented in early charters and has variations like *Brooker* or *Brookward*, meaning " by the brook." *Abovebrok* is a name appearing in the Hundred Rolls.

Mor or *More* also is recorded in the same document. From this we have the well-known names of *More* and *Moore*, and in addition a shortened form of *Atte-Moor* in *Amore*. Our forefathers were fond of telescoping words in this fashion as the reader will see in the further examples that follow. There are also compounds of *Moor* in *Morcombe* and *Moorman*.

Yard and *Hurst*. *Apelyard* and *Apelgarth* of early records still flourish and multiply in our modern directories as *Appleyard* and *Applegarth*. Coster and custard apples were grown in the " yards " and " garths " of our ancestors. *Ashhurst* is one of the many compounds of *hurst* a wood, like *Lyndhurst* the wood of linden trees, *Elmhurst* of elms, *Ashurst* of ash trees, *Hazlehurst* of hazel trees. We have of course also the names *Hurst* and *Hirst* from the same source.

Field. From the older form *atte Feld* we get *Field* and *Fielder ;* as well as *Atfield* and *Attfield* by joining the preposition to the noun. From *de la field* we have also *Delafield.*

Transport difficulties in Medieval times were many, and the most serious of them resulted from the breakdown of bridges. The lords of neighbouring manors were responsible for the maintenance of these. To recoup them for the expenses thus incurred they were allowed the privilege of erecting toll gates and levying dues on traffic that crossed the bridges. The second part of this contract they performed with assiduous care and levied tolls on footpassengers as well as heavy ox-carts that passed over these flimsy structures. But all too often they failed to apply the money thus collected to the maintenance of the bridges so that the history of these is one of constantly recurring disaster.

Sometimes the task of keeping the bridges in repair fell to the lot of the hermits, who took their station at the bridge-ends and invited the charity of passers-by.

The *Bridgeman*, who was in charge of the bridge ; the *Briger* who constructed or repaired it, and the man who dwelt at the *Bridgend* were people of some consequence. *Bridgeman* and *Bridger* like *Fielder* are names of occupation and have no place in the category we are dealing with, but *Bridgend* is a local surname.

In the old records we find such names as *Stephen atte Brigende, John Bridgeman, John Bridges* and *Roger del Brigge*, the forerunners of *Bridgend, Bridger* and *Briggs,*

Hay. From *Hay*, *hey*, O.E., *hege*, a hedge, we get in the simple form the surnames *Hay*, *Haye*, *Hayes*, *Haigh*, and *Hawes*. There are several compound forms as *Haycraft* (hedged croft), *Broadhay*, *Haywood*, *Heywood*, *Hayley*, and *Lyndshay* (or linden hedge). *Lyndshay* has now become *Lindsay* and *Lindsey*.

Churchgate. *Churchgate* is also the present form of *Chirchyate*. The second element in this name *yate* or *yat* is still commonly used in the northern counties for *gate*, O.E., geat, a gate. From the simple form we have the surname *Yates*, and there are many compounds.

Churchestighele, which occurs in the Writs of Parliament, has been shortened by usage into *Churchstyle*.

Ford. Except for the dropping of a final *e* this name has come down to us unchanged. It is an element in numerous compound place names. For the Saxons, unlike the Romans, were not bridge builders, and very often formed their *tuns* or village settlements near the fords or rivers. From the names of these townships like *Oxen-ford*, *Chelmsford* and *Guildford* we derive many surnames.

Gore. Both *Gore* and *Goreway* are names mentioned in the Hundred Rolls, but the latter is now probably obsolete. A *gore* was in former days the name for a triangular piece of land. From this we may infer that the original *Gores* and *Goreways* were the owners or occupiers of such a property.

Greenslade. This is one of the numerous compounds of *slade* which in early English means *dale*. It has many compounds as in *Waldeslade*, meaning the wooded valley (cf. German *wald*, wood), *Morslade*, the valley by the moorland, *Oakslade* from *Oeslade* as well as *Green-slade*.

Hill and *Hull* are from the old forms *Hil* and *Hulle*. Both mean *hill*.

Howe. A *brow* or small hill is represented in early records by *atte Howe, de la How,* and *ad le Ho.* *Howes* is the genitive form.

Lea. In its many forms probably the most popular of local names. It appears in our directories, as in old records, in many forms, *Lee, Lees, Leas, Leigh, Laye.* There are numerous compounds as *Hindley, Harley, Cowley, Horsley* and *Shipley.* As we see from these names, the hind, the hare, the cow, the horse and the sheep found pasture on these meadow lands. But it was through the last of these, the sheep, that England first amassed wealth and became a great trading nation. Though England in the middle ages had trouble enough in the quarrels of the feudal barons and civil war, it was in comparison with the rest of Europe, peaceful, and the only land where sheep breeding could be safely carried on. Hence the trade in English wool that came from the sheep bred on the leas of this country. This wool was famous throughout Europe and the merchants of the Staple who at first controlled the trade provided the English kings with a large proportion of their revenue. As Eileen Power has said in her *Medieval England* the woolsack on which the Lord Chancellor sits in the House of Lords is as full of pure history as the office of the Lord Chancellor itself, and " reminds a cotton-spinning, iron-working generation that the greatness of England was built up, not upon the flimsy plant which comes to her to be manufactured from the far East and West of the World, nor from the harsh metal delved from her bowels, but upon the wool which generation after generation has grown on the backs of her black-faced sheep." From this we can see that the *lea* or pasture land, as the source of our national wealth was all important. The word originally meant " a clearing " and is from M.E. *lay, ley*, untilled land. A Saxon leah, lea (gen. léage) a lea. Cognate with Low German *loge*, Flemish *loo*, as in Waterloo.

Sale. From French *salle* (sale) a hall (Cotgrave) indicated at first the principal room in a castle or mansion. Our forefathers in the Middle Ages had rudimentary ideas about domestic architecture. For centuries after the Conquest the greater houses were divided into four or five rooms. In addition to the *sale* or hall there were the kitchen, which in its turn was subdivided, and the *solar*, afterwards known as the parlour. The *solar* was the private room of the lord where he lived and slept. The whole household, except the lord and his lady ate their meals in the hall, and also slept there. It was the common living room of the house, and it was of such importance that it become synonymous with the house itself. This arrangement persisted for three centuries, when with more subdivisions of space the sale or hall declined in importance and became a vestibule. But the name was then very often given to the house itself. So it is probable that Alexander and John Sales took their names from the houses near or at which they lived. Thus we have such names *Geoffrey atte Kitchen* and *Richard ate Parlour*. *Parlour* if not obsolete is certainly very rare, but *Kitchen* survives and flourishes in *Kitchin*, *Kitchen*, *Kitching*, and *Kitchingman*. The descendants of the *gate-man* are our *Yeatmans*, while the servant in charge of ale and wines has enriched our stock of names with *Sellerman*.

Spitels. The names *Richard ate Spitele* and *Gilbert de Hospitali*, which occur in the Writs of Parliament and the Hundred Rolls respectively require little explanation. The present forms of the name are *Spittal* and *Spittle*. In the *Calendarium Inquisitionum Post Mortem* we find a name with the same meaning in *Idonia de la Fermerie*. This has developed into *Fermor* and *Firmer*. Every Abbey and Monastery had its *fermery* or *spital* until the reign of Henry VIII, and from these the names originated.

Stone. A.S. *stàn*, a stone, is a name frequently found in the records, especially in compounds. From these we have the names *Stonehouse*, *Stoneclough*, *Stoneham*, *Stoneley*, *Stones*, *Stoney*, as well as *Stone*.

Street. In *William atte Strete* the name *Strete* or *atte Street* would be useless as a means of identification nowadays, but in Medieval times it was otherwise. The country was but sparsely populated and there must have been hundreds of townships with single streets of only a few houses. The name was then an easy way of distinguishing its owner.

Shaw. Just as *Shaws* or wooded shelters for livestock abound in every country district, so the name *Shaw* which represents it is to be found in all localities. It is also found in many compounds as in *Openshaw*, *Berkenshaw* (birchwood), *Crankshaw*, *Bradshaw*,

Grimshaw and *Langshaw*. Our ancestors used patience and observation, if not much imagination in finding surnames for their fellows. Every institution and landmark were made use of for this purpose—the bury or thorp, the well, the trees that surrounded the manor house, the wayside cross, the stone house that the prosperous smith had built, or the wooden hut of the serf—all were employed in the great work of collecting the material for future directories.

Bury or Borough

Thus the bury itself was represented in the Hundred Rolls by *John atte Bury*, and from this and other entries in ancient records, our present day *Burys*, *Atterburys*, *Boroughs*, *Burrows*, *Burgs* and *Borrows* may learn that their fore-runners were people of some consideration in those primitive townships of long ago, and remember with modest pride that in the struggle for English freedom, the men of the boroughs were foremost in the fight.

The Well

To the community situated far from river or brook, the well as the source of its water supply was important enough to provide a surname for the family that lived nearest to it. We are accordingly not surprised to find such names as *Wells*, *Atwell* (from *Atte-Well*) *Weller* and *Wellman* making a brave show in local directories. *Weller* and *Wellman* are names of occupations.

TREE NAMES

Ash. Before a name beginning with a vowel, *atte* becomes *atten* as in *Roger atten-Ash,* from which we have the aphetic *Nash* as well as *Ash.* Time has modified the compound *Ashlegh* into *Ashley.* Another interesting surname from ash is *Fiveash,* while the compound *Asquith* is equivalent to *Ashwood. Nokes (atte Noke)* is shortened from *Atten-oak.* Just as " a nadder " has lost its initial letter and become " an adder," so here we see the opposite process, and the noun has gained an initial letter at the expense of the preposition. So that from oak we have the names *Oak, Oakes* and *Nokes,* while there are many compounds, e.g. *Oakden* the oak valley, *Oakeley, Oakeshott, Oakenfold, Oaker, Oakey, Oakley, Oakhill* and *Oakwood.* The surname *Snooks* is a contraction of " seven oaks."

But the contributon of *oak* to English surnames does not end here. Oak, M. Eng. *Ook* is from Anglo-Saxon *àc.* From this source we have the names *Acland* and *Acton.*

The Rowan-tree. The principal names derived from this tree are *Rowntree* and *Rownthwaite.*

The *Holly,* O.E. *hollyn* gives us *Hollis, Hollins, Hollingworth, Hollingsworth, Hollings.*

In addition to these already dealt with there are other trees that have given us surnames, notably the elm, beech, alder and lind. From elm we have *Elmhurst* and *Elmer* ; from beech, *Beech,* as well as the occupative names *Beecher* and *Beechman* ; from alder, *Alder* and *Nalder* (from *atten-alder*) ; from the linden *Lind, Lynd,* and several compound names.

Throp or *Thorp*, a small village. This word, now archaic retains its vitality in the names *Thorpe*, *Thorp* and *Thrupp*. It is also an element in many compounds, e.g. *Buckthorpe*, *Calthrop* and *Winthrop*.

Names like *Garth*, *Fell*, *Pike*, so prevalent in Cumberland and Westmoreland serve to remind us that the Scandinavians who ruled the Isle of Man also occupied these counties. *Garth* is a Scandinavian term for yard or enclosure and in its simple form may be seen in many directories. It is also an element in many compound names, as *Hogarth*, and the name of a former President of the United States, *Garfield*.

The name *Fell* was borne by the subject of the famous epigram :

> I do not like thee, Dr. Fell,
> The reason why I cannot tell,
> But this I know, and know full well,
> I do not like thee, Dr. Fell.

Fell is also found in several compounds the most popular of which is *Grenfell*.

From *Cliff* we have *Cliffe* and *Clift* and *Clive*. It has many compounds the most famous of which is *Wycliffe*, White Cliff. Others are *Radcliffe*, *Redcliffe* and *Sutcliffe*.

Pike or *Peak*. A common name for a hill-top offers several monosyllabic surnames, as *Pike*, *Peake*, *Peek*, *Peck*, *Pick*.

Cross or *Crouch*. People in the Middle Ages liked to see symbols of their faith, and the Church saw that their needs, in this respect at least, were fully satisfied.

Crosses were to be found in every township however
small, before the great religious houses and by the wayside. Like everything else distinctive, these crosses or
crouches served the purpose of nomenclature. In the
Hundred Rolls the names of *Jordan ad Crucem*, *John
atte Cruche* and *William de la Rude* (Rood was the old
English name for cross) may be found. From these
we get the names *Cross, Crouch, Rood, Rudd* as well
as *Croucher* and *Crouchman*.

Tun or *Ton*. We have considered bury as a source
of surnames and must now turn to *ton* which originally
meant a farmstead but now signifies *Town*. It is
mostly used in compounds which indicate its position
or tells who its founder was. There are as Canon Taylor
says in his famous chapter on Village Names, 32 tuns
that have retained the name of Middleton from which
we gain the surname. We also have surnames from
Upton or " the higher tun," *Eaton* or " the tun by the
river," *Morton* or a " tun on or by a moor," *Fenton* " by
a fen," *Dalton* " a tun in a dale," *Denton* " in a dene or
dale," *Compton* " in a combe," *Clifton* " near a cliff,"
and *Chilton* " by a spring " from the Norse *Keld*, a
spring.

There are many of these tuns scattered over the
forty counties of England, and the majority of these
have yielded surnames, as well as place names.

Sale or *Seal*, meaning a hall or chambered house,
give us two surnames, one of French and the other of
Saxon origin, *Sale* and *Seal*.

Cot, a Cottage. From *Cot*, a cottage, come many names
simple and compound. In the Hundred Rolls there

are several including Richard and William *Coteman*, William le *Cotier* and Beatrice *Cotewife*. William *Coterel* may also be seen in the Writs of Parliament. From these we have the modern names *Cotman*, *Cotter*, *Cotterel* and *Coates*. In compound names there are *Draycott*—from *Dregcota*,—the dry cottage, *Cottingham*, *Cottridge* and *Alcott*.

The *Mill*. At all the larger manor houses in Medieval times there was a mill (Latin *Molina*, a mill) to which the tenants were compelled to bring their corn for grinding. This custom caused much dissatisfaction as the small holders complained that the Reeve took more of the corn than was his due. From *Mill* we get the surnames *Mill*, *Mills*, *Milne*, with the occupative names *Milner*, *Miller* and *Mellor*.

Spence. We have had *Parlour* and *Kitchen*. Here we have *Spence*, a very common name in the north of England meaning a pantry, larder or store-cupboard, Mid. English *Spence*, botery. In Scotland *Spence* is the common name for larder, while the occupative name *Spencer*, an aphetic form of dispenser, means one who spends, or distributes provisions.

Mews. In the Telephone directory may be found the names *Mew*, *Mewes*, *Mews*. In these days Mews harbour sports models and other kinds of motor cars. They also shelter horses and even sometimes fashionable people who love to parade the fact that they are leading the simple life. But in olden times a *Mewe* was a coop in which hawks were kept when moulting. The word is from the French *muer* to moult, Latin *mutare* to change. In the *Squire's Tale* Chaucer has the lines

And by hir beddes heed she made a mewe,
And couered it with velouettes blewe,
In signe of trewthe that is in wommen sene.

Hearne. A common name in the records is *Hurne* or *Herne*, which like *Wyke* and *Wray* have the meaning of " corner." A compound of *wray* gives us *Thackwray* meaning the corner where the thatch was kept. From this the ancestors of the novelist derived their family name of *Thackeray*.

Meadows. From meadows we have the names *Mead* and *Meadows*, as well as the compound *Meadowcroft*.

Dike. The dikes that divided these fields furnish us with *Dykes* and *Diker*. Dike has sometimes the opposite meaning to ditch and stands for a mound.

Streams. From streams we have the surnames *Rivers*, *Brook*, *Brooks*, *Beck*, *Burns*, *Fleet* meaning a creek (Mid. Eng. *flete* to float, swim). There are many compounds of these as in *Brookland*, *Brookman*, *Brookwell*, *Brookward*, *Brooksbank*, *Brookside*, *Beckford*, *Beckett*, *Beckham*, *Beckley*, *Beckton*, while the surname *Troutbeck* reminds the tourist of a well-known mountain stream.

Fosse. From the French *Fosse* the names *Foss*, *Fosse* and *Foskett* (foss-gate) are derived. While *Fossett* stands for fosse-head.

PLACE NAMES FROM PERSONAL NAMES

In the Eleventh Chapter of his book on *Words and Places* Canon Taylor has pointed out that in most countries and particularly in England, Germany and France local names are in large measure derived from personal names. As many of the Norsemen and Saxons who settled in England bestowed their own names on the land they occupied many of the names of our villages or tons offer a vague but permanent memorial of the hardy adventurers from the north who drove the native Britons from their lands, or made clearings in the forests and settled by wood and ford. The names of many of these enterprising pioneers are preserved in early documents. In these ancient writings some of the names through long usage have been strangely changed from their original forms. Others have suffered scarcely any modification. Thus the Norman Mowbrays gave their name to a Yorkshire plain, the Vale of Mowbray as well as Melton Mowbray in Leicestershire. The Northumberland Percys who derived their name from an obscure French hamlet gave it to the manors of Bolton Percy and Wharram Percy in Yorkshire, which belonged to them before they became Earls of Northumberland, and Wardens of the Scottish Marches.

The village of Ashby in Leicestershire belonged, from the twelfth to the fourteenth century to the *La Zouch* or *Such* family. From them it received the name of *Ashby de la Zouch*. About the same time that the Zouches took possession of Ashby a gentleman with the picturesque local name of *Richard de Rivers* acquired Stanford in Essex. Since then the village has been known as *Stanford Rivers*. In the same neighbourhood the parish of Wellingate passed into the hands of Hervey of Spain (de Ispania). Through this circumstance it took the more imposing name of Willingale Spain.

Stanton Harcourt in Oxfordshire gained its name from Robert de Harcourt into whose possession it passed by marriage seven centuries ago. A *Cheney* gave his name to the manor of *Cheney Longville* in Salop. Hinderskelfe in the North Riding of Yorkshire became Castle Howard, when Charles Howard the third Earl of Carlisle became its manorial lord.

With the aid of Domesday Book it is sometimes possible to discover the personal names of the Scandinavian founders of ancient settlements, and as Taylor explains in the interesting chapter already mentioned Edington was the tun of *Edwin* and Addlethorpe the thorp or village of *Ardulfr*, and Woolsthorpe that of *Ulfstone*. Anlaby took its name from *Olafe*, *Ganthorpe* from *Gamel*, *Sewerby* from *Siward*, *Thorkelby* from *Thorkill*, *Amerby* from *Edmund*, and *Ellerby* from *Alward*, while Osmaston in Derbyshire was the tun of Osmund.

These are but a few examples from Canon Taylor's long list, but they are enough to show that personal names have made some return for the many raids which those in search of surnames have made on the Gazetteer.

WORDS DERIVED FROM SURNAMES

Many surnames having acquired special significance have been borrowed by the Dictionary from the Directory and are now current counters in the verbal exchanges of everyday intercourse. It has been said that no German has ever reached real popularity among his compatriots until a herring has been called after him. This mark of high distinction was earned by the Iron

Chancellor after the Franco-German War of 1870-1, since when the " Bismark Herring " has been a favourite dish in Germany. In the same way boot-makers in the earlier era expressed the nation's joy at its deliverance from the Napoleonic peril, and incident-ally did a good stroke of business by selling their wares as Bluchers and Wellingtons. The brougham named after the famous lawyer has gone a little out of fashion since the advent of motoring, but the word has been in common use for a hundred years, and seen much service. The *Spencer*, the short coat invented by a Lord Spencer of the eighteenth century is no longer worn, but the term still survives and may again be as popular as it was with our grandparents. A contemporary of this Lord Spencer was Lord Sandwich, who first gave us that make-shift meal beloved of tourists and conferred his name on it. Lord Sandwich was an inveterate gambler, and it is said sometimes remained at the gaming table for twenty-four consecutive hours without retiring for a regular meal. On these occasions he instructed his servants to prepare him slices of beef put between layers of bread. With these he renewed his flagging energies. A wit of the period wrote the following epigram about these inventive noblemen :

> Two noble earls, whom, if I quote.
> Some folks might call me sinner,
> The one invented half a coat,
> The other, half a dinner.
> The plan was good, as some will say
> And fitted to console one,
> Because in this poor starving day
> Few can afford a whole one.

The brothers Gobelin gave their name to the world famous tapestries, and the equally renowned Macintosh which owes its origin to an enterprising tradesman at Charing Cross, still weathers storm and tempest, and considering the uncertainties of our climate the term is not likely to be ousted from our vocabulary until some other kind of rain defying dress is invented. To one Greek philosopher we owe the term *platonic*, so beloved of old fashioned novelists and to another the adjective *epicurean*.

Through *Dr. Banting*, a pioneer in the art of slimming, we get the verb " to bant."

The word *derrick* has an interesting history. It is now used for a kind of crane by means of which sunken ships are raised. In Elizabethan days it meant the gallows or hangman and was named from a Dutch executioner. Blount in his *Glossographia* (1656) says " *Deric* . . . is with us abusively used for a Hangman because one of that name was not long since a famed executioner at Tiburn." Dekker in *Seven Deadly Sins of London* (ed. Arber p. 17) says " I would there were a Derick to hang up him." The name Derrick=Dutch *Dierryk*, *Diederik*, and answers to the German *Dietrich*, Anglo-Saxon *Thēodrīc*, " ruler of the people."

The inventor of that murderous instrument known as the guillotine was a Dr. Louis. At first it was known as the Louisette, and so for a time it remained almost unknown. But among those who saw it was a Dr. Guillotin, a member of the Convention, and he was so impressed by its efficiency that he introduced a Bill authorising its use. In this way he gave his name to the machine that Danton and Robespierre used so freely, but which now is used for the more innocent purpose of paper cutting. *Martinet* a diminutive form of the name *Martin* (from Latin Mart—the stem of Mars) was the name of a French officer under Louis XIV who was supposed to be a strict disciplinarian. Hence the common use of the word.

The verb to *macadamise* we owe to a John Macadam who a century ago, introduced a new method of road paving. Galvanism is named from the Italian scientist, Galvani of Bologna. We derive the word *pinchbeck* from a London watchmaker, *Chr. Pinchbeck* who specialised in cheap jewellery.

We speak of an expurgated book as *bowderlised*, since Dr. Bowdler published an edition of Shakespeare from which all coarse or objectionable expressions had been deleted.

About half a century ago an Irish landlord, Capt. Boycott had a dispute with his tenantry. In consequence of this the tenants agreed together to have no dealings with him. The word *boycott* passed at once into the language, and anyone who has since received the same treatment has been spoken or written about as having been *boycotted*. *Mesmerise* and *mesmerism* are named after the celebrated German physician *Mesmer*, who flourished in the second half of the Eighteenth Century.

The *doily*, a small napkin, is said according to the *Spectator*, No. 283, Jan. 24, 1712, to be named after " the famous Doiley."

What is known as Lynch Law is a form of punishment

inflicted by mobs in the Southern States of America on negroes who have been guilty of crimes. This form of punishment was first popularised by Charles Lynch, a Virginia planter (1736-96).

The verb " to burke " meaning to murder by suffocation, has passed out of general use though it still holds pride of place in English Dictionaries. It is from the name of Burke, an Irishman, who earned money by suffocating his neighbours and selling their corpses to the doctors.

CHAPTER IV

PATRONYMICS

> We could scarcely have a single lesson on the growth
> of our English tongue, we could scarcely follow up one
> of its significant words without having unawares a lesson
> in English history as well, without not merely falling on
> some curious fact illustrative of our national life.
>
> —TRENCH, *The Study of Words*.

THE Baron or Franklin who held his land in fee took his
surname from his estate. The villager took his from
some landmark or feature of the country-side. The
stranger was identified by his place of origin. Others
received nicknames or were known by their trade or
craft. Still another class, and amongst these must have
been some with pride of ancestry, took the personal
name of the father or other relative. It is with this
class we have now to deal.

Family names formed in this way are among the
most widely distributed of our surnames. After all, it
was perfectly natural that a man whose name had been
formally entered in an early Roll as John, filius William
should take the surname Williamson, or that Robert the
son of *Dick* should become *Dickson* or *Dixon*. Many
examples of family names formed in this way could be
given, for these are taken not only from the names
themselves but from their shortened and pet forms as

well. Thus from David alone there are *Davidson*, *Davison* (Davyson), *Dawson* (Daw's son). Some take the genitive form with the added " s," and have the same meaning, as in *Davis*, *Davies*, and *Dawes*. Thus in addition to *Richardson*, *Phillipson*, *Johnson* and *Jonson*, we have also *Richards*, *Phillips* and *Jones* expressing the same relationship.

The Welsh *ap* preceding a font name also means " son of," as in *ap Madoc*, the son of Madoc, and *ap Evan*, the son of Evan.

The Normans also used the prefix *Fitz*, the old French form of *fils* to denote the same relationship, of which the names *Fitzgerald*, the son of Gerald, and *Fitz-clarence*, the son of Clarence, are typical examples.

Baptismal names provide an unmistakable index of popular sentiment. They wax and wane in popularity today as they did centuries ago. The name of a king who has won the allegiance of his subjects as well as those of his family, is faithfully copied and transmitted to the next generation of his people. A great feat of arms by land or sea, the triumph of some statesman, the prowess of a mighty cricketer, and the skill and courage of heroes of the prize-ring are all commemorated at the baptismal font. During the Boer War names like Buller, Baden-Powell, Methuen, Mafeking and Ladysmith were conferred on helpless infants ; while only a few years ago large numbers were christened Jellicoe, Beatty, Haig and Lloyd George.

The baptismal name *William* was a favourite with the followers of the first two Norman Kings. Of this the early records supply abundant evidence. One of the most popular surnames derived from it is *Williams*, which is borne today by many thousands of people, and enjoys special popularity in Wales. Other familiar derivatives are *Williamson*, *Will*, *Wilson*, *Willson*, *Willis*, and *Wills*. There are also from pet forms *Wilkins*, *Wilkes*, *Wilkinson*, *Wilcox*, and *Wilcockson*. From the French equivalent Guillaume, with an added diminutive we get *Guillemot*, *Gillot*, and *Gillett*. Then there are *Bill* and *Billson*. But these have a double origin, and some, at least, of them are occupative and indicate the Bill-maker.

After the death of William II the name William declined in popularity and John became first favourite with the English people. If evidence of this were wanting it would be abundantly supplied by the number of people who at the present day answer to the surname *Jones*. Mark Twain, many years ago noticed that in his own country the name *Jones* occurred almost as often in the Directories as that of Smith. So he dedicated one of his early books to " *John Jones*," and explained that as the person to whom a book was dedicated was expected to buy a copy, he expected a princely revenue from this work.

But the popularity of the name John in England owed nothing to royal favour, for the sole bearer of it among our Kings was justly regarded by his people as a treacherous and contemptible coward. Whatever the cause *John* is one of the commonest names in Christendom. Our name *John* Bull corresponds to the French *Jean* Crapaud and the Russian *Ivan* Ivanovitch, " the

embodiment of the peculiarities of the Russian people "
as Wheeler observes in *Noted Names of Fiction*. The
names of characters in our nursery rhymes, *Jack* Horner,
Jack and Jill, and *Jack* Sprat provide evidence of the
popularity of the name as well as such phrases as " Jack
of all trades," and " Jack's as good as his master."
The name has been given to implements such as smoke-
jack and boot-jack, and we have names like Jack-a'-
lantern, Jack Pudding, Jack-o'-lent, John-a-dreams.

> Yet I, a dull and muddy mettled rascal, peak
> Like John-a-dreams unpregnant of my cause.
> HAMLET.

It may here be remarked that though *Jack* is generally
used as a pet substitute for *John* the question of its
origin remains insoluble. It is possibly due to the
diminutive form *Jankin*, though there is little doubt
that it has been confused with the French *Jacques*, a
name freely used in France. *Jaques* is from Latin
Jacobus=Greek 'Ιακωβος, =Hebrew *Ya'agob*, Jacob ;
literally " one who seizes by the heel."

John is from Anglo-French Johan ; Latin, *Johannes*,
Greek, Ιωάννης, Hebrew, Yehōkhanān, Yokhānān, lit.
" God is gracious."

Jacques and *Jaques* are both English surnames.

The surnames derived from the font name *John*
are greater in number than any others in English
Directories. Of these *Johns, Jonson, Johnstone, Jenkins,
Jones, Jenks, Jennings, Jean, Jeans,* and *Micklejohn*
are but a few taken at random. The German and
Flemish form *Johannes*, shortened to *Hans*, has also

embedded itself in our nomenclature in the form of the diminutive surnames *Hankin* and *Hancocks*.

Though not so prolific in derivatives *Jack* is nevertheless very well represented by the well-known surnames *Jack, Jacks, Jackson, Jacox*.

It will be seen from the above examples that surnames have been formed from the pet and shortened forms of a font name, as well as from the name itself, and that there is a great variety of these pet forms. Some of them are formed by rhyming as in Bill and Will ; Hob, Dob and Rob (Robert) ; Rick, Dick, Hick, Rich, Hitch and Higg. Others are shortened forms. Tim for Timothy ; Day for David ; Chris for Christopher ; Gil and Gib, Gilbert, but also for the French *Guillaume* ; Bat and Bette for Bartholomew.

In Colle for Nicholas, and Tolley from Bartholomew we have pet forms taken from the second syllables of names.

To many of these shortened forms the diminutive suffixes *ie, y, kin* as well as the French *et, ot*, are added. The last two in English often become *at*.

Robin was a pet name for Robert, but it was also a proper name of high renown, for it comes through French from O. High German *Ruodperht* (German, Ruprecht, i.e. Rupert). It means " fame bright," " illustrious in fame." The pet name *Hob* is from *Rob*, a shortened form of *Robert*.

From Robert and its pet forms come a great many surnames. From Robert there are *Roberts, Robertson, Robertshaw ;* from Robin—*Robins, Robinson, Robin, Robinet, Robison, Robson*, and the name, with a double

diminutive *Robotkin;* from *Hob*—*Hobbes, Hobbis, Hobbs,
Hobbins, Hopps, Hopkins;* from *Hodge*—*Hodgson,
Hodson, Hodges, Hodgetts, Hodgins, Hodgkin, Hodgkins,
Hodgkinson*; from *Dodge*—*Dodson, Dodgson, Dodge;*
and from *Roger*—*Roger, Rogers, Rogerson, Rodgers,
Rodgerson, Roget.*

Though Richard Cœur de Lion spent only a few
months of his reign in England, he was the most popular
of the Angevin Kings, and in after years, like Robin
Hood, he became a hero of romance, and many wondrous tales of his prowess and bravery were current
among the peasantry. In consequence of this his name
and its variants Rick, Hick and Dick were freely used
at the font, and so helped to swell the list of surnames.
The names from this source alone run into hundreds,
which a reader who is interested can easily discover for
himself by a little research. Here are a few. From
Hick and Hitch we find *Hick, Hickes, Hickey, Hickie,
Hicking, Hickman, Hickmott, Hicks, Hickson, Hitch,
Hitchcock, Hitchcox, Hitchen, Hitchens, Hitchin, Hitch-
ings, Hitchins, Hitchman.*

From Rich and Rick we find *Rich, Riche, Richelle,
Richens, Richford, Richman, Rick, Rickaby, Rickard,
Rickards, Rickatson, Rickell, Rickerd, Rickett, Ricketts,
Rickman, Ricks.*

We have seen that font names wax and wane in
popularity. Some that were once fashionable are now
no longer used. Others that were almost unknown in
the Middle Ages flourish exceedingly. The canonisation
of St. Thomas of Canterbury and of St. Hugh, the child
martyr of Lincoln, made these names popular, though

the derivatives from them are comparatively few. From Thomas come the surnames *Thomas, Thompson, Thomason, Thom, Thomasson, Thomerson, Thomson, Tom, Tomkin, Tomkins, Tomkinson, Tompkins, Tompkinson, Tompson, Toms, Tomsett, Tomson.*

These variations on a well-known name illustrate the popular indifference to spelling by the scribes of the Middle Ages.

The legend of St. Hugh which Chaucer has told with such grace and tender pathos through the mouth of the Prioress was already known to the most ignorant bondman of the period. The name became popular and the surname survives in various forms, the best known and most obvious of which is *Hughes.*

In Wales we find aphatic forms of *ap Hughes,* in *Pugh* and *Pew.* Similar changes are from *ap Howell* to *Powell ; ap Rees* to *Preece* ; *ap Henry* to *Penry* ; *ap Harry* to *Parry* ; *ap Owen* to *Bowen* and *ap Evan* to *Bevan ; ap Robin* to *Probyn ; ap Richard* to *Pritchard ; ap Enion* to *Benyon.* Of font names that were once popular and are now all but forgotten there is one of historic interest. This is *Amalric,* varied forms of which are *Americ, Emeric, Ermeric.* In its Italian form *Amerigo* it was the font name of the explorer *Vespucci,* who after a notable voyage across the Atlantic found a new country and called it by his name. In English Directories this font name survives in *Amar, Amery, Emery, Emerson, Emberson, Imeson, Imray* and *Imrie.*

The Norman font name *Hamon* is no longer used for baptism, but its memory is perpetuated by the surnames *Hamon, Aymons, Hammond, Hamneson.*

Coupled with the Norman French diminutive *et* we
have *Hamonet*, and the shortened form *Hamnet*,
which in its turn became a common font name.
Hamnet was the name of Shakespeare's son who was
also known as Hamlet like his godfather Hamnet or
Hamlet Sadler, a tradesman of Stratford-on-Avon.

Gilbert in early times was one of the commonest font
names, and in its contracted form *Gib* was the general
name for a male cat.   In Sherwood's *English-French
Dictionary* appended to Cotgrave appears the definition
" A *gibbo* (or old male cat) Macon."   Graymalkin was
the female cat.   In I Henry IV I, 2, 83 (Shakespeare)
" I am as melancholy as a gib cat," and in Chaucer's
Romaunt of the Rose, 6207 : " Gibbe our cat,"

That awaiteth mice and rattes to killen.

In Gower's poem on Wat Tyler's rebellion, among the
Thommes, Symmes, Dawes, Juddes and others who are
called to their leaders' banners is Gibbe—" Betteque,
Gibbe simul, *Hykke* venire jubent."   From this con-
traction there is a long list of surnames—*Gib, Gibb,
Gibbens, Gibberd, Gibbes, Gibbin, Gibbings, Gibbins,
Gibbon, Gibbons, Gibbs, Giblin, Gibney, Gibson.   Gilbert*
the full name, is also well represented.

The surnames from *Gil* have a mixed ancestry as
some of them are from *Giles*, and the French *Guillaume*,
which has diminutive offshoots in the surnames
Guillemin and *Wuillemin*.   From *Guillemin* comes the
shortened form *Gilman*.

But the confusion does not end here.   *Gilpin* undoubtedly represents *Gil* the pet form of Gilbert,

but is also a local name, derived from a mountain beck in Westmorland.

Again as Professor Weekley has pointed out, that though French settlers in England made *Gilbert* a popular surname, its origin is English, and it comes from the Anglo Saxon *Gislbeorht*. But there is still another *Gil* of Gaelic origin, Gaelic, *gille*, a boy or servant ; old Irish *gilla*, a servant, from which Skeat derives the word *gillie*, a common name in Scotland for a page or servant. From this form we have such surnames as *Gilchrist*, servant of Christ, and *Gilmour*, big servant.

Thus we see names beginning with *Gil* may come from anyone of five sources. The origins of many names are so obvious that the student, new to the subject, is often tempted to be rash and take names at their face value. But this is to court disaster. Tracking names to their hiding places is great sport, but the hunter who gets heated by the chase and is rash and impetuous, too often misses the quarry and courts disaster.

The English people never took kindly to the name *Henry* and the only surnames formed directly from it are *Henry*, *Henryson*, *Henri*, *Henery*, *Hendry* and *Henderson*, and these are more frequently met with in Scotland than elsewhere. But Harry, the pet form, achieved enormous and wide-spread popularity. The omission of the *n* and broadening of the vowel in Henry was more suited to the English tongue, and in old plays the Kings of that name are all spoken of as *Harry*. In Shakespeare's Henry V, the French King and his envoy Mountjoy both speak of their enemy as *Harry*, while at the end of his spirited address to his soldiers before Harfleur, the English King exclaims :

> I see you stand like grey-hounds in the slips
> Straining upon the start. The game's afoot,
> Follow your spirit, and upon this charge
> Cry, " God for Harry, England, and St. George."

Of the surnames derived from Harry, *Harris* is one of the seventeen that may be found in every county of England. *Harrison* is almost as widely distributed ; so that the enterprising American publisher who has been inviting all members of the Harris family to subscribe for a large book that contains the history of that famous clan has a wide field for his enterprise.

Other surnames from this source are *Harrie, Harriot, Harries, Hariss* and *Harrisson*.

From *Bat* one of the pet forms of Bartholomew we have the surnames *Bates, Batson, Badman, Batty, Batt, Bateman*. But of these, *Batt* is sometimes a nickname and *Bateman* occasionally occupative.

The other form *Bet* yields *Betts, Betterton*, though these may also be matronymics and descend from Beatrice.

In *Toll* also from Bartholomew we get *Toler, Tolson, Tolley*.

Jordan and its nickname form *Judde* survive in the surnames *Jordan, Judd, Judkins, Jukes*, the sharpened form *Jutson* and *Jutsum*.

Lawrence had four pet forms as Law, Lay, Low, Lawrie and from these came the names *Law, Lawson, Lawman, Lay, Lowe, Lowes, Lawrie*.

Lay is also local, and indicates residence at or near a lea or meadow.

Wat is the shortened form of the Norman French *Wautier, Walter*. From these we get the names *Watts, Watson, Walters, Waters, Waterman* and *Walter*.

Piers or *Pierce* the variant of Peter was a common font name in the Middle Ages, but it has not made many contributions to the list of surnames. The most notable of these are *Pearce, Pearse, Pears, Pearson*.

Colle, the shortened form of Nicholas, is responsible for *Collis, Collins, Colley, Collinson, Collings*.

From Nicholas we have *Nicholson, Nicklin, Nickling, Nickinson* and *Nicklinson*.

One of the famous font names of the period, a family name of the Angevin Kings was that of *Fulk*. Every Frenchman in England held the name in high honour. For were our Kings not descended from Fulc of Jerusalem, that military genius and mighty warrior who had subdued the Norman barons and wrested one half of the fairest French provinces from the rule of France ? After the accession of Henry II and for more than a century afterwards the name was very popular in England, but considering its vogue it did not leave many derivatives. Amongst these are the surnames *Fewkes, Vokes* and *Foakes, Fulker, Fulkes, Fulcher*.

Of the famous warriors of ancient times the name that was most frequently heard at the baptismal font was that of Alexander the Great. Indeed his name was popular throughout the then known world, and was also perpetuated by several of the cities he founded and which bear his name. The walls of the chamber of the Queen of Henry I at Nottingham were painted with scenes from Alexander's stirring history.

But the interest in the name in England was lukewarm beside that shown for it by the Scottish people, who adopted it as their own in much the same way as Germany claims Shakespeare today. In Italy the name is *Alessandro*, and the contracted form *Sandro*. In Scotland the shortened forms are *Saunders* and *Sandy*. In the Highlands the name was modified to *Alaster* and then to *McAlister*. From the English form the surnames *Alex*, *Alexander* and *Alexandre* are derived.

The Scottish have given us more, *Sandall*, *Sanders*, *Sanday*, *Sandell*, *Sandels*, *Sandelson*, *Sandeman*, *Sander*, *Saunders*, *Sanderson*, *Sandle*, *Sandler*, *Sandon*, *Sands*, *Sandy*, *Sandys*. But *Sandeman* may also be for messenger, from *sondes-man* " a messenger," from A. S. *Sond*, *Sand*.

Bertram, though English in origin, was not a well known personal name in England till after the Conquest and has scarcely altered in form since. *Berteram, le Barbur's* name, was entered in the Hundred Rolls in 1273, but the name has left very few derivatives. From the contracted form *Bert* we have *Bert*, *Bertie*, *Bertin*, *Berton* ; and from the full name *Bertram* and *Bertrand*.

Baldwin. This name is not among the first sixty of our surnames, but it is widely distributed and is found in most of the modern Directories. After the Norman Conquest it enjoyed especial favour and was patronised by royalty. Its vogue is explained when we know that an aunt of William I married Baldwin, the Earl of

Flanders, and that the Conqueror himself married Matilda daughter of the fifth Earl. At that period Flanders was known as Baldwin's Land.

Ball was a favourite contraction of this name, and has yielded the surnames *Ball, Ballard, Baldin, Baldie, Balding, Bald*. But *bald* is for Middle English *balled*, and as Skeat and other etymologists point out, the original meaning of the word was " shining or white," as in " bald faced stag," i.e. a stag with a white streak on its face. Then the word developed the meaning " hairlessness," as the obvious quality of a hairless head was its shining quality. In C.T. Prologue, *l* 198 we find

His head was *balled*, and schon as any glas.

Also it was, according to Wyclif's version of the Scriptures, the cry of the impertinent young Israelites " Stay up ballard " that called down the wrath of the outraged prophet. But *Ball* is also a shop-sign nickname ; and in the Western Counties it is also the term for a small field, so that it is in some cases local.

Taking these facts into account it is clear that *Ball, Ballard, Baldie* and *Bald* have only a limited application as personal names and that generally they have come into existence as nicknames.

Of Randolph the usual pet nickname in early times were *Ran, Randle*. In Cheshire Randle was immensely popular through the famous Crusader Randle, Earl of Chester, who was the chief land-holder in the county. From those the surnames *Randle, Randall, Randell, Rand, Rands* ; with the diminutive *kin, Rankin, Ranken* ; and also *Rank* and *Rance*.

Herbert was one of the Teutonic font names that the Normans made familiar in England. In the year 1000 A.D. St. Heribert was Bishop of Cologne. This and other circumstances made the name very popular in England in the Twelfth and Thirteenth Centuries. In our own time the name has been truncated in unrefined circles to *'Erb*, but in the surname period, our forefathers found it, like other Teutonic names, too imposing to trifle with. It is possible that some of its bearers answered to the contracted form Bert but as this would cause them to be mistaken for the other Berts, whose names were shortened from *Bertram*, *Cuthbert*, *Albert* or *Hubert*, it is unlikely that such a pet form would be given. From the full name we get the surnames *Herbert*, *Herbertson* and *Herbison*.

The English *son* and genitive *s*, as well as the Welsh *ap* have been referred to as used in patronymic formations. A word or two may now be added about the Gaelic *Mac* with which Scottish, Manx and Irish personal names are prefixed. *Mac* like the Irish O', and the French *Fitz* means " relative of." *Mac* has been retained in many Scotch and some Irish names but the O' in Irish is gradually falling into disuse. In a Special Report on Surnames in Ireland published in 1894 and issued by the Stationery Office in 1909 as a Blue Book the following are said to be the most popular names in the sister isle, *Murphy, Kelly, Sullivan, Walsh, Smith, O'Brien, Byrne, Ryan, Connor, O'Neill, Reilly, Doyle, MacCarthy, Gallagher, Doherty, Kennedy, Lynch, Murray, Quinn,* and *Moore*. Of these only two retain the *O'*. There are a considerable number of Irish names prefixed with *Mac* the most popular of which is MacCartney from *Cart(h)annach*, " the charitable."

Among Manx names *MacCubban*, " son of Cubbin," Cubbin is a mutation of *Gibbon*. *Clucas* is an aphetic form of MacLucas, " son of Luke," *Quilliam* of *MacWilliam*.

Among well known Scottish names, the awkward looking *Colquhoun*—quite easy when pronounced correctly as *Coohoon*—is local. It was assumed by Umfridus de Kilpatrick when he acquired the lands of Colquhoun from the Earl of Lennox in the reign of Alexander II.

MacArdle stands for " sons of Ardghal " and means " mighty of valour." *MacAulay* is Celt and Scandinavian and means " son of Olaf." *MacBeath* and its variant *Macbeth* signify " son of life " from *beatha*, " life." *MacConechy* is the son of *Douchard* or *Duncan*. *MacGowan* is the " son of the smith," while *MacIlrath* means the " son of the grey servant." *MacIntosh*, *MacIntyre* and *MacLaren* represent the sons of the chief, the carpenter, and Lawrence respectively, and MacLean, which stands for *Mac-gille-eoin*, means " son of the servant of John," *Eoin* is the genitive of the nominative *Jain*, John.

MacNair (mac-au-aighre) is for " son of the Heir," and *MacNish* or *Neish* is for " the son of Angus " *Macfie* or *Macphee* has the poetic if slightly obscure interpretation " son of dark of peace."

MacWalter needs no elucidation, but it may be explained that in addition to *MacWilliam* there is also the unaccountable *MacWilliams* with the genitive *s* as

well as the *Mac*.   But among surnames there are many
of these freak forms which are due to popular usage.

The Gaelic name *Adair* is local and means " dweller
at the ford by the oak tree," which is as picturesque an
address as the heart of poet could desire.

A curious name found principally in Scotland
Gemmel, is from old French *gemel*, meaning *Twin*, which
is also an English surname.   There are also *Bairnsfather*, *Barnfather*, which still survive and *Childesfader*
now no longer used.   *Fairchild* and *Fairbairn* still
flourish as also does *Dawbarn* (David's child).   Other
names indicating relationship are *Widdows* and
Widdowson ; from the names spelt *Cosin* in old rolls
we have *Cosens*, *Cousins*, *Couzens*, *Couzyn*.   Both
Brothers and *Frere* are still in use, as are also *Father*
and *Fathers* though none of the four are well represented in the Directories.   Son is represented in the
London Telephone Directory by *Soan*, *Sons*, *Soans*,
Soanes, and in the same list are also *Uncles* and *Eames*,
the latter from Middle English *eme*, uncle.   Spenser in
the *Faery Queen* spells the word *eame*, while in the *Prompt.
Parvulorum* its definition is as follows, " *eme*, *fadiris
brodyr*."   *Neave* and *Neves* for nephew (M. English
Neve, nephew) also *Parent* and *Kinsman*.

Some of these names are elements in many compounds which will be dealt with later.

The names in the above paragraph, which needless
to say are not patronymics, are dealt with in the
chapters on nicknames.

CHAPTER V

Prophets, Martyrs, Warriors

> I create you
> Companions to our persons, and will fit you
> With dignities becoming your estate.
>
> Cymbeline.

A considerable number of English surnames come to us from Scripture history, from the tales of minstrels, ancient legends, and from the saints whose virtues were contemplated with awe and reverence.

The peasant of the Middle Ages was ignorant and unlettered. He knew little of the sacred writings, and such acquaintance with them as he had was derived from mystery plays or the sermons of the preaching friars, and confined to the more striking incidents in Bible history. He was naturally interested in the story of the Creation and the lives of the early Patriarchs as told in the book of Genesis. The stories of Abel and Samson moved him to pity and sorrow. The exploits of Joshua and David stirred his martial spirit. The deeds of Solomon, Elijah and Samuel roused him to amazement and the trials of Job evoked his sympathy. The figures in the New Testament that inspired his devotion were those of John the Baptist, the disciples of Jesus Christ, St. Paul and, of course, the Virgin Mary.

About all these he knew something, and this scanty knowledge influenced him when selecting names for his children.

It was to these peasants and their more tutored neighbours, in the long vanished centuries that we principally owe the long list of Biblical surnames that crowd our Burgess Rolls and Directories. Many of these, naturally, belong to people of Jewish birth, but many more who bear the names of Abraham, Isaac, Jacob, Abel and their many derivatives are unmistakably of English birth.

Adam as its many varied forms show, was a favourite name with the English people. The most familiar surnames that it has given are *Addis, Adcock, Addyman, Adams, Addams, Adamson, Addamson, Addy, Adkin, Ade, Ades, Adey, Adie, Adkins, Adkinson, Atkinson.* But there are many more.

Richard Rolle de Hampole was an Augustine monk who wrote a poem, *The Pricke of Conscience*, in the Northumbrian dialect in 1340, in which he accounts somewhat quaintly for the names Adam and Eve :

> For uunethes (scarcely) es a child born fully
> That it ne bygynnes to goule (howl) and cry ;
> And by that cry men knaw than
> Whether it be man or weman,
> For when it is born it cryes swa (so) ;
> If it be man it says " a, a,"
> That the first letter es of the nam
> Of our forme-fader (forefather) Adam.
> And if the child a woman be,
> When it es born it says " e, e,"
> E es the first letter and the hede
> Of the name of Eve that bygan our dede.

Joseph gives the surnames *Joseph*, *Josephs*, *Josephson* and *Josephy*.

Abraham is represented by *Abram*, *Abrams*, *Abraham*, *Abrahams*, *Abrahamson* and many derivatives, though some of these also represent *Abel*.

David has in its derivatives a cloud of witnesses to its amazing popularity as a font name—*Davies*, *Davis*, *Davidson*, *Davison*, *Davy*, *Daw*, *Dawes*, *Dawe*, *Dawson*, *Dawkins* and many more.

The story of *Jacob* and his many tribulations appealed to the English people, who despite their lack of idealism possessed imagination and a keen sense of drama. The name of the patriarch was assumed in many forms and the effect of this may be noted in the following surnames which however only represent a small proportion of those that have been formed from this popular patronymic, *Jacob*, *Jacobs*, *Jacobson*, *Jacobsen*, *Jakins* and *Jakes*.

The name *Job* also made its appeal and appears among surnames in various guises, the most notable of which are *Jobson*, *Jubb*, *Jupp*, *Chubb*, *Jobling*, *Jobbins*, *Juby* and *Jupe*.

Ely, *Ellis*, *Elliot*, *Ellison* are alternatively from Elias or Ellen. *Eales*, *Ealey*, *Eley*, *Elias*, *Elieson*, *Elles* and *Ellett* are other examples.

Though often adopted as a font name *Solomon* has left very few variants among surnames, its chief contributions being *Solomons* and sometimes *Salmon*.

If the number and diversity of derivatives be the best test of popularity, the name of the prophet Daniel certainly stands very high among the great figures of the

6

Old Testament, for few are perpetuated by more surnames. Amongst these are *Daniel, Daniels, Dann, Danson, Dance, Danielson, Dancock*.

The use of Peter or Piers as a font name presents a curious problem. Among the Apostles he was the most vivid and striking figure. His name is intimately linked up with the Gospel story. He founded the Church in Rome and the throne he established there has since been held by an unbroken succession of Popes.

Yet the name though used with some freedom, especially in its French forms Pierre, Piers and Pierce, was by no means so favoured at the font as John, William and Thomas. The name was freely used in the scanty literature of the period by William Langland and the unknown author of *Peres* the *Ploughman's Crede* and others. The ploughman in common speech was known as Piers as was *Davie the Diker*, just as *Hodge* typifies the agricultural labourer today.

Peter and its derivatives in both its English and French forms make a substantial contribution to the list of English surnames. Among them we find *Peter, Peters* and *Peterson* as also the diminutive *Peterkin* and *Peterkins*. As in early English *s* and *c* were frequently interchanged two surnames are spelt *Pearce* and *Pearse*. *Pears* is generally an imitative form of the French equivalent *Pierre*, though sometimes it stands for a fruit nickname. In *Pierce* the vowels are transposed and *Pierre* presents the French form unchanged. Other forms are *Piers, Pierson, Petre*. Among the diminutives are *Petrie, Perry, Perkin, Perkins, Perks, Perret, Perrett, Perrott* and *Peron*. *Perowne* is probably a lengthened form of the last named. *Peto* and *Pierre-pont* are local names. *Peto* (*Peitou*) is taken from Pritou and *Pierrepont* from Pierrepont.

From *Noah* come the surnames *Noyes, Noy* and *Noys*; and from *Moses, Moss* and *Moyes* as well as *Moses* and *Mosses*.

We have no surnames that can be definitely associated with Pharaoh and Potiphar. But it is possible that _Farrow_ may represent the King of Egypt, and *Pettifer* the name of his chief officer. But these are merely guesses. What is certain is that *Pettifer* is in some cases a nickname and represents *Pied-de-fer* " foot of iron."

Both the English Matthus and the old French Mahieu are among the names from Matthew. These include *May, Makin, Makins, Makinson, Mason, Mathes, Matheson, Mathew, Mathewes, Mathews, Mathewson, Mathey, Mathias, Mathius, Mathiason, Mathiasen, Mathieson, Mathieu, Mathieux, Mathuen, Mathys, Matkins, Matson, Matt, Matterson, Mattey, Matthes, Matthew, Matthewman, Matthews, Matthewson, Matthias, Mattheason, Matthys, Mattinson, Mattison, Matts, Mattson, Mayall, Mayell, Mayes, Mayhew, Mayo, Meekin, Mee, Meakins* and *Meeson*. Not only are there many names from *Matthew* but some of them have crowds of representatives that take up many pages of the Directories.

The second evangelist, Mark, has bequeathed us the surnames *Mark, Marks, Marsh, Marcus, Marcock, Marson* and *Markin*. But the first and third of these are local names and represent a mark or boundary, and *March* is also a place of origin, and denotes two villages one English and the other French which had their fame extended through their adoption as surnames.

Luke is a more adaptable name and has left us a more generous supply of surnames. From this font name we have *Lucas*, *Lucis*, *Luck*, *Luckett*, *Luckie*, *Luckin*, *Lucking*, *Lucks*. Other derivatives are *Lucock*, *Locock* and *Lockett*.

Surnames from John have already been given in an earlier chapter.

The name Simon or Simeon was borne by many of the characters that flit across the stage in the moving pageant of Biblical story, and it is natural that a name so often recalled should make a deep and lasting impression on the public mind. So we find the names *Sim*, *Simkin* and even *Simonet* recurring in ancient rolls. Today it takes more various forms and appears as *Simms*, *Sims*, *Simpkins*, *Simpson*, *Simmons*, *Simonds* and *Symonds*.

That famous ascetic of the fourth century, St. Anthony, has left us a reminder of his virtues in *Tonson*, *Townson* and *Tonkins*, which are aphetic forms of his name. Monks of the Monasteries dedicated to this saint were permitted to leave their pigs feeding in the streets and the pigs were known as *Tantony* pigs.

From St. Cuthbert the surnames *Cuthbert*, *Cuthbertson*, *Cutbeard* and *Cobbet* come. Cobbet was originally *Cowleytson* or so it appears in a record of the fourteenth century.

St. Lawrence's career, it is said, ended unpleasantly. His persecutors who loved a spectacle put him on a gridiron over a slow fire. This martyrdom made him extremely popular. From him we get the names *Larkin, Larson* and *Lawrence.*

The many Flemings who came to England after the Conquest heralded the renown of St. Lambert, the patron saint of Liege, who suffered martyrdom in the eighth century. *Lambert* is the French form of *Landbeorht* meaning " land-bright." The surname *Lambie* is a diminutive of Lambert.

In the ancient records the name appears as Robert Lamberd (Rolls of Parliament), and Lambekin Taborer (Issue Rolls). The lineal descendants of these are besides *Lambie* and *Lambert, Lampson, Lampkin* and *Lambkin.*

St. Paul, too, has made his contribution to the roll of English surnames. In the fourteenth century when surnames were being adopted by the peasantry as well as the ruling classes the name Paul had a broader pro-nunciation than now. Langland in *Piers Plowman* spells it " Powel," and Chaucer in the Prologue of the Nonne Pristes Tale has :

"Ye," quod our hoste, "by seint Poule's belle,
Ye seye ryght sooth; this monk, he clappeth loude, . . ."

To this form the surnames *Powlson, Pawson* closely approximate. We have also *Polson* as well as the in-dubitable *Paulson.* In addition to these there are the diminutives *Poulett, Powlett, Paulett, Pollitt.*

Philip the apostle bore a Greek name that lent itself easily to the formation of pet forms. It became, for this and other reasons very popular. In the time of Henry

VIII Skelton the poet laureate varied his onslaughts on Cardinal Wolsey in *Why Come ye nat to Courte ?* and other poems, by writing a delightful elegy on the death of a pet bird, *Phyllyp Sparowe.* In Skeats' larger edition of *Piers the Plowman* (B-Text) the editor has noted that where other MSS. have a totally different line, the Oriel MSS. have the line

Schulden go synge scruyseles with sire philip the sparwe.

Philip has left many surnames and amongst the best known of these are *Philips* and the more extended *Philipson.* There are also *Phipson* ; the genitive forms *Phipps, Philps* and *Phelps,* and the diminutives, *Phillot, Philcox* and *Philpot.* The last name meaning little Philip was a favourite name with the early French settlers as we discover from the records. Here we find the names Thomas *Phylypotte,* John *Philipot* and John *Philypot* in the *Calendar. Inquis. Post Mortem,* the Munimenta Gildhallæ, and the Rolls of Parliament respectively. Through similarity of sound *Philpot* also becomes *Fillpot,* which has its place in more than one Directory. The letter of Careless to Philpot which Archbishop Trench quotes emphasises the association of the two names " Oh, good Master Philpot which art a principal *pot* indeed, *filled* with much precious liquor, oh, pot most happy ! of the High Potter ordained to honour."

In the early registers we find the names *Felip, Felyp,* as well as *Filpot* and *Fylpot.*

But the derivatives from *Philip* do not end here. *Pott* and *Potts,* aphetic forms of *Philpot,* make a brave show as surnames in Borough Rolls, while the diminutive *Potkin* may also be found.

Andrew, the patron saint of Scotland, like Philip bore a Greek name, meaning " manly." But this name, like that of their own patron saint, St. George, made little appeal to the English people. But the Scots took very kindly to it and used it freely though they did not abbreviate or form pet names from it possibly because they esteemed it too highly. The principal surnames from it are *Andrew*, *Andrews*, *Anderson* and *Anderton*.

The name of the first of the martyrs, *Stephen* was naturally in great favour in Plantagenet days and of this the early records supply abundant evidence. In these we find the names *Stephen le Fox*, *Stephen le Bar*, Jordan fil. *Stephen*, Robert *Stevene* and *Esteven Walays*. From these have come our modern *Stephens*, *Stevens*, *Stivens*, *Stephenson*, *Stevenson*; also the contracted *Stinson*, *Stimson* and the diminutive forms *Stennet* and *Stennett*, *Stenning* and *Stephany*.

Clement was one of the outstanding figures among the early fathers, and his name was adopted by several of the Popes. It was also held in honour by the English people and used freely as a font name. Its shortened forms *Clem* and *Clim* were almost as familiar as Robin, Dick or Gil. Clim o' the Clough, the outlaw who ranged the Cumberland forests near Carlisle was second only in renown to Robin Hood himself and was the hero of more than one popular ballad. The principal surnames derived from it are *Clements*, *Clemson*, *Clementson* and *Clemens*. It is also found in compounds like Clemsha (Clems Shaw), and in a famous French name we have the diminutive *Clemenceau* meaning little Clement.

Though many font names had been adopted from sacred history, some of them as we have seen from the names of saints, none were taken directly from the Bible. They were derived principally from the mystery and miracle plays and pageants which had so powerful an influence on popular thought during the Middle Ages. To these old plays reference will be made in another chapter.

No English version of the Bible was available, and the people were too ignorant to make use of it if it had been.   Many of the clergy were unable to read or write.

But change was coming fast.   The teaching of Wycliffe and his followers, the Peasants' revolt, the invention of printing, the Renaissance with the establishment of Grammar Schools and rise of the Universities, the publication of Coverdale's Bible under Royal authority, all produced an amazing change in the spirit and temper of the English people.   With the rise of Puritanism England became, as J. R. Green says, "the people of a book, and that book was the Bible." Except for the mystery plays and the little known poems of Chaucer, the people knew nothing of literature, and it was a notable occasion when a great concourse of people gathered at St. Paul's to listen to the reading of the six Bibles which Bishop Bonner had ordered to be set up there.   From then onwards the book became the standard of the English language and hundreds of its phrases coloured everyday speech.   Among its many influences its effect upon nomenclature deserves notice.

Before the translation of the Bible became common property only the outstanding names, and especially those connected with picturesque incidents in Scripture history were known to the people. But after that event the names of the major and minor prophets as well as many others that only a careful student of the Bible might be expected to know, became common Christian names. In the records of the sixteenth century may be found such names as Gamaliel, Emanuel, Abigaill, Reuben, Amos, Zabulon, Gideon, Abacucke (Habakkuk), Melchizedek, Ezekiel, Esdras, Sydrach, Judith, Isachar and Seth.

In old records many entries furnish evidence of this change. Among them we find the names Shadrach Luke, Thomas Matthew, George Job, Samuel Scripture, Ananias Dyce, Zacheus Ivitt, Caleb Morley, Aquila Wykes.

For a time at least these Scriptural names did not displace old favourites, Richard, William and Gilbert were as popular as ever. The only difference was that parents had a greater choice in selecting names for their children.

But as the influence of the Puritans spread from the middle and professional classes to the common people, religious persecution fanned the popular enthusiasm into fanaticism ; and this persecution welded the sectaries together into one compact body, which stubbornly resisted the tyranny of Charles I and his government. Many of the more fanatical assumed religious texts and mottoes as Christian names, which were as banners flung from the outer walls and proclaimed their religious and political faiths. The names that had done duty for centuries fell under a ban. In the eyes of the zealots these were tainted with popery or paganism. In all matters sacred as well as secular they took the Bible as their guide. As Macaulay says in his *History of England* (c. i.) " In such a history it was not difficult for fierce and gloomy spirits to find much that might be distorted to suit their wishes. The extreme Puritans, therefore, began to feel for the Old Testament a preference, which perhaps they did not distinctly avow even to themselves, but which showed itself in all their sentiments and habits. They paid to the Hebrew language a respect which they refused to that tongue in which the discourses of Jesus and the Epistles of Paul have come down to us. They baptised their children by the names, not of Christian saints, but of Hebrew patriarchs and warriors."

Names like Joshua, Hephzibah, Zerubbabel, Enoch, Hiram, Phineas and Hezekiah are frequently met with in Parish Registers. The fashion began with the Puritans, and such names are still to be found occasionally. The writer of this book has relatives who bear the names *Grace* and *Faith*.

But the most curious are those that express the humility or self scorn of their bearers. One that appears in the State Papers (Domestic) is that of *Milcom* Groat. As Bardsley points out *Milcom* stands for the abomination of the children of Ammon. Other names of this class include *Cain, Abner, Delilah, Tamar, Korah* and *Sapphira*. Then there were the abstract names that expressed the religious zeal of their bearers. Camden gives a short list of those that flourished in his own day, and among these are *Reformation, Free-gift, Earth, Dust, Ashes, Delivery, More-Fruit, Tribulation, More Trial, The Lord is near, Discipline, Joy again, From above.*

Camden explains that these and similar names " have lately been given by some to their children, with no evil meaning, but upon some singular and precise conceit."

The classic example of this kind of name is *Praise-God Barebones.* But the brother of the gentleman who bore this singular name answered to another that was even more remarkable. He was called *If-Christ-had-not-died-for-you-you-had-been-damned-Barebones.* But this was too great a mouthful, especially for his more irreverent acquaintances and he was generally known by the last name only, and he figures as *Damned Bare-bones* in the history of those troubled times.

In his book on *Surnames,* Lower quotes the following from the registers of Warbleton :

Bapt. 17 Dec. 1609 *Flie-Fornication*, the base son of
Catrus Andrews.

    1617 *Be-stedfast Elyarde*
      "   *Good-gift Gynnings*
    1622 *Lament Willard*
    1624 *Defend Outered*
    1625 *Faint-not Dighurst*
      "   *Fere-not Rhodes*
    1677 *Replenish French*

In Walker's *Sufferings of the Clergy* mention is made of the Rev. Accepted Frewen who became Archbishop of York and died in 1604. The Archbishop's brother was named *Thankfull* Frewen.

This subject of Puritan font names has been dwelt on at some length principally because of its effects on American nomenclature. Those who examine the lists of names of the Pilgrim Fathers who sailed to the New England States, and compare them with the names of the emigrants who went to Virginia and Maryland at once notice a difference. Among the latter there are very few Puritan names. For the men who first attempted to form a colony by the James river were adventurers and men of broken fortune who were drawn to the New World by the marvellous stories of the gold and other precious metals to be found there. Afterwards their ranks, depleted by Indian massacres, famine and sickness, were filled up by prisoners of war and indentured apprentices, many of whom had been kidnapped.

But the people who sailed in the *Mayflower* and the fleet of ships that followed it to the New England States were the victims of religious persecution and they bore names that proclaimed their faith. These and similar names they handed down to succeeding generations. The persecutions they suffered and the hardships and privations they endured in the new settlements made them cling the closer to the names that were the symbols of their faith. Since those far off days many millions of Europeans have chosen America as their home, and the swelling tide of emigration still flows westward, but those original settlers in Massachusetts and New Hampshire have never been submerged. They can still be identified by the baptismal names their ancestors adopted when Puritanism first became a force in Elizabethan and early Stuart times. They rarely used any but Old Testament names such as David, Gideon, Abel, Abraham, Daniel, Asa and Lot or abstract terms as Patience, Charity, Grace, Faith, Hope, Prudence and Mercy. The Anglo-Norman names that were favourites with our common ancestors and even the new Testament names like James, Simeon, Peter and Matthew are not often used. The old New Englanders have the same taste in font names as Cromwell had when choosing his troops. As Cleveland said of the Lord Protector and his Ironsides : " Cromwell hath beat up his drums clean through the Old Testament, you may know the genealogy of our Saviour by the names of his regiment.   The muster master hath no other list than the first chapter of St. Matthew."

CHAPTER VI

Matronymics

Knowing this, that never yet
Share of Truth was vainly set
   In the world's wide fallow;
After hands shall sow the seed,
After hands from hill and mead,
   Reap the harvests yellow.—Whittier.

When Canon Bardsley's *English Surnames* was published more than half a century ago, the critics of some of the religious papers, with the assurance that ignorance sometimes breeds, stoutly maintained that matronymic surnames had no existence save in the author's imagination. Others were shocked with Bardsley for suggesting that our rude forefathers were no better than they should be, and that some bearers of a respected name might have among their remote ancestors some woman of light virtue. This, of course, seemed very dreadful to Mrs. Grundy and her tribe, and the poor author was bespattered with abuse for daring to publish evidence in support of his statement, evidence that he had been laboriously collecting for years.

Had the critics gently pointed out some of Bardsley's many errors, they would have served the good cause of truth, and the author would have been grateful. But instead they attacked him where he was firmly entrenched on the rock of truth, and he had little difficulty in blowing their fine spun theories to the winds.

No one now is so ignorant and foolish as to contend that there are no English matronymics. There are plenty of them and the honour of first demonstrating their existence belongs to Canon Bardsley.

How did these matronymics arise? Some writers as Bardsley says, have not " hesitated to affirm them to be wholly of illegitimate descent." But this is just as foolish as to assume that the English people from the twelfth to the fourteenth century were immaculately virtuous.

There was, of course, much immorality in those centuries as there has been in every succeeding one, and as there is today. But it is none the less true that children were often given, or themselves assumed their mothers' names for other reasons than illegitimacy. In the Middle Ages a child born after its father's death always took the name of the mother. When children were adopted by women they were frequently given the names of their foster parents. It is also not difficult to understand that where a strong minded woman was the real head of the household, the children who looked to her for guidance might also take her name. In the fifteenth century surnames were assumed and changed with an ease that seems astonishing to us. Thus as mentioned in Chapter I, a document of the year 1441 shows that in one family the elder brother took the local name of Asheby. His. brother became Adam *Wilson*, and Adam Wilson's son called himself John *Adkynson*. Another extract quoted in the same chapter mentions the sons and grandsons of Ydo Towter as named Nicholas *Pudding*, Richard *Marshall*, Diccon *Smith*,

Jopson and *Rogerson*.   May not one of these have taken
the name of the mother ?

In T. F. Thistleton Dyer's *Old English Social Life* as
told in the Parish Registers, we get some strange and
illuminating glimpses of the past.   As the author says,
the Parish Register is no respecter of persons, for " on
its pages are enrolled, side by side, the names of the
high and low, rich and poor."

In these we find many entries of the birth of illegitimate children.   As in the register of Allenborough cum
Bramscote, Nottinghamshire, we find that " upon
Sonday the 18th November, 1560, was born Joan yᵉ
infant of Dorothie begotten in fornication, christened
at home by reason of weakness."

The terms Children of God or Creatura Christi were
often applied to illegitimate children, which throws
light upon the passage in *Piers Plowman* :

> I conjured him at the laste
> If he were Cristes Creature
> Anoon me to tellen
> " I am Cristes Creature " quod he ;
> " In Cristes Court by knowe wel,
> And of his kyn a party."

But many thousands of helpless babes had not even the
doubtful advantage of sharing their mothers' names,
but were left to the tender mercies of that stern step-
mother the parish.   All the London parishes, and
doubtless many others had many foundlings left on
their hands and were often in difficulties when names
had to be found for them.   Thus in the Temple registers
between 1728 and 1755 one hundred and four foundlings

were baptised there all of whom were named *Temple* or
Templar. In St. Lawrence, Jewry the name *Lawrence*
was invariably given to foundlings in that parish. But
in some parishes no regular system seems to have been
used. For the register of St. Dunstan's, London,
shows

1618 Mary Porch, a foundling bap^t 18 Jany.

1631 Eliz. Middlesex, found in Chancery Lane.

Mr. Dyer also quotes from the register of St. Dionis
Backchurch an entry of December 14, 1567, which runs
as follows : " A chylde that was found at the strangers
dore in lymstrete, which chylde was fownde on saynt
petters day *in An° d'ni* 1567 and fonde of the p'ishe
coste, wherefore they named the chylde by the day that
he was fownd, and syrname by the p'ishe, so the chyldes
name ys *Petter Dennis*."

A similar system of nomenclature was adopted in
hundreds of other parishes and by this source alone the
sum of local surnames was greatly augmented.

Crabbe, the poet, in his humorous poem *The Parish
Register*, relates the story of Sir Richard Monday, of
Monday Place, who began life as a foundling. The
lines about this successful man are as follows :

> To name an infant met our village sires,
> Assembled all, as such event requires.
> Frequent and full the rural sages sate,
> And speakers many urged the long debate.
> Some harden'd knave, who rov'd the country round,
> Had left a babe within the parish bound.
> First of the fact they questioned, " Was it true ? "
> The child was brought—what then remained to do ?
> " Was't dead or living ? " This was plainly proved,
> 'Twas pinched—it roar'd—and every doubt remov'd.

Then by what name th' unwelcome guest to call
Was long a question, and it pos'd them all.
For he who lent a name to babe unknown,
Censorious men might take it for his own.
They look'd about, they ask'd the name of all,
And not one Richard answered to the call.
Next they inquir'd the day, when passing by,
Th' unlucky peasant heard the stranger cry ;
This known, how food and raiment they might give
Was next debated, for the rogue would live ;
At last, with all their words and works content,
Back to their homes the prudent vestry went,
And Richard Monday to the Workhouse sent.
Long lost to us, our man at last we trace,
Sir Richard Monday died at Monday Place.

From the facts set out it is clear that a considerable proportion of illegitimate children, the foundlings, do not appear among the metronymics ; and that of those who do come within this category, a large number, no blot attaches to their names. In any case it matters very little, for at some period in every family the inevitable black sheep appears, and very few of those who know the history of their line, for twenty generations back, have little reason to be proud of them.

Matronymics. The font name *Jane* is comparatively modern. Before the Tudor era *Joan* was universal. Then, as Camden says, " some of the better and nicer sort misliking the former (Joan) turned it into 'Jane.' " The Marriage of Henry VIII with Lady Jane Seymour made the name fashionable, and Joan was left to the serving wench and the peasants' daughters. At the present time we are witnessing a revival of some of the old names, and as Joan looks distinguished and aristocratic, it enjoys special favour. But those who bear it may be interested to know that it was in the early days one of the commonest of baptismal names.

The close resemblance of John to Joan and of the French form Jean to its corresponding Jenny or Jennie, led inevitably to confusion. Johnson and Joanson, as they were bound to do coalesced, and at least a few of the *Joneses* must have owed their origin to Joan. In like manner it is impossible to discriminate between the *Jennings's* and *Jennison's* derived from *Jean* and *Jenny*. Similar confusion exists between Jack and Jacqueline, though the surname *Jacklin* is clearly from the latter.

In the Hundred Rolls may be found the following entries *Alicia* fil. *Sisselot*, Bella *Ceaselot*, Hugh *Sauzaver*, in the Rolls of Parliament Richard *Sisselson*, and the *Testamenta Ebor*, John *Sisson Syssat* Wilson and John *Sissotson*.

These are from the favourite Christian name Cecilia and its derivatives. This name was popular with all classes and assumed many forms. We learn from history that William the Conqueror's daughter was baptised Cecile. Sis and Cis were the popular shortened forms of the name. A popular seventeenth century song has :

> Joan *Siss*, and Nell shall all be ladified,
> Instead of hay carts, in coaches shall ride.

Langland's version of the name in *Piers Plowman* is

> *Cesse* the souteresse.

The names *Sisselot*, *Sissot* and *Cesselot*, quoted above are variant diminutive forms of the same name. From these together with *Sisselson*, *Sisson* and *Sissetson* our modern *Sissons*, *Sysons* and *Sisselson* are derived.

Another Norman font name that figures largely in the long roll of surnames is Emma. Curiously enough it came to England before the Conquest through the marriage of Emma, the daughter of Richard I of Normandy to Ethelred the Unready. In old records it is generally spelt Emme, and also takes the diminutive forms *Emmot* and *Emmet*.

According to one of Bardsley's critics Emmot is a form of Amyas and therefore a masculine name. Bardsley had no difficulty in demonstrating the absurdity of this claim. He pointed out that *Emmot* is *always* Latinised as *Emmota*, and that in old marriage licences Richard de Akerode gets a dispensation to marry *Emmotte* de Greenwood (Test. Ebor III, 317), and Roger Prestwick to marry Emmote Crossley (ditto 338).

From this name then we get the surnames *Emmett*, *Emmot*, *Emson*, *Empson*, *Emmes* and *Emmotson*. *Emmet* is also sometimes an insect nickname from Emmet, an ant, Mid. English *emete*, *amote*.

Through St. Petronilla the name Petronilla, the feminine of Peter, became popular with the peasantry in the Middle Ages. But in later years the name lost caste, as it was used to indicate a type of woman to whom the term Magdalen is now applied. But it still lives among our surnames as *Parnell*, *Parnwell*, *Pernel*, *Pernall* through its pet forms Parnel and Pernel.

In its extended form *Amabilia*, the name Mabel was in common use in Norman times, and the pet forms Mabel and Mab were familiar as household words. From Mab originate the diminutive surnames *Mabbett* and *Mabbott*, the genitive *Mabbs*, *Mabbes*, as well as *Mabson* and *Mabe*. There are also *Mabey*, *Maby*. A sharpened form gives the names *Mapp* and *Mappin*.

To Chaucer as to everyone else in the fourteenth century the female font name Constance was known as *Custance*, and old records offer convincing evidence of its popularity. These also make us familiar with its shorter forms *Cus* and *Custe*. From these the surnames *Custance*, *Cuss*, *Cust*, *Cussons*, *Cussens*, *Cussen*, *Cussans*, *Custerson* and *Custins*.

The pet form *Beton* from Beatrice has also provided a number of modern surnames like *Beaton*, *Beton* and *Beatson*.

The name *Dulcia* and its variants *Douce*, *Dulce* and *Duce* yield the surnames *Dowse*, *Dosset*, *Dowsing*, *Dowson*, *Dowkin*, *Doucett* and *Dowsett*.

The more homely form of Lætitia, Lettice has placed among our surnames *Lettice*, *Lett*, *Letts*, *Letson* and *Letty*. The ladies whose names were inscribed Theophania in the old registers by Anglo-French clerks, would have been greatly astonished if their friends and acquaintances had greeted them by such a name. To these and everyone else they were known as Tiffany. This name in its turn has given us the surnames *Tiffany*, *Tiffen* and *Tiffin*.

Eleanor or Alianora has left us a multitude of pet names, and these in their turn contributed a proportionate number of surnames. From the first form of the names the commonest variations were Elinor, Ellen, Lina, Nell, Linot, and of the second Annora, Alinot and Annot.

These give the surnames *Eleanor*, *Ellen*, and in some cases *Nelson*. But the last name is also derived from *Neil's* son.

Juliana like Eleanor took many shapes. As Julian it acquired popularity which grew as it also became Gillian or Gilian or again Julyan. Its fame spread still further when these were shortened to Gil and Jill and so were immortalised in nursery literature.

Though Jack and Jill are associated and contrasted in a hundred poems and ballads it is the connection between Gilbert and Jill that mostly concerns the student of nomenclature, for the surnames from these sources are naturally much confused. The Celtic *Gil* and derivatives from Guillaume also add to this confusion.

A notable diminutive of Juliana is Juliet or Gilot, while a further contraction is *Juet*, from which our surname *Jewitt*, and through northern dialect pronunciation *Jowett*.

In Matthew xiii. 45, of Wickliffe's translation of the Scriptures occur the words, " The kyngdom of hevenes is lyk to a marchaunt that seekith gode *margarites*, but when he hath found one precious margarite, he went and solde alle thingis that he hadde, and boughte it." Here Wickliffe uses, as he does elsewhere the term *margarite* for pearl, which in the Middle Ages was the common name for this jewel.

The name Margaret then, the meaning of which everyone naturally understood, quickly became a favourite, and Marjorie and Margot, which were its pet forms became the names of thousands of English girls. Magot, Madge and Meg were other forms of this name. Surnames from this source are *Maggs*, *Margots*, *Maggots*, *Margetts*, *Margetson*, *Margerison*, *Margison*, *Meggs* and *Megson*. From the same name the French have the surnames *Margot* and *Margoten*.

From Mary, which strange to say was little used in the early centuries in England, the only pet form is the diminutive Mariot from which the surnames *Marriot* and *Maryatt*, which correspond to the French names *Mariette* and *Mariotte*.

Isabel though not greatly in favour was shortened in popular usage to *Ib* and *Ibby*. The former of these with the French diminutives added has left us the surnames *Ibbot* and *Ibbet* and *Issot*. Other names from this source are *Ibbs*, *Ibbotson*, *Ibson*, *Ibberson*, *Ibbetson* and *Ibbitson*.

Then there is the pet form *Bell*. From this come the names *Bellet* and *Bellot* and *Bell*.

But the surname *Bell* is not merely a diminutive of *Isabel*. It comes from at least two other sources which probably accounts for its great popularity. It is a local name, and indicates a dweller near the Bell, and a nickname for one who lives at the sign of the Bell. " John atte Belle" is mentioned in one of the Camden Society's publications. It is also a nickname for someone fair or handsome, Mid. English *belle*, O. French *bel*. In the Hundred Rolls there is *Peter* le *Bel*, and in Writs of Parliament Richard atte Bell.

Chaucer in *Troilus and Creseide* sings

> Good aventure O *bele* nece have ye
> Ful lightly founders, and ye conne it take.

Bellis and *Bellin* are not from the diminutive Bell, as some have supposed. *Bellis* is an apheric form of ab-Ellis, the son of Ellis.

Bellin is local from the French village Bellon or Belleau, meaning the fair water. It is Latinised in the old records as *de Bella Aqua*.

The " Sybby Sole, mylke wyfe of Islynton," mentioned in Cocke Lorelle's Bote, bore the famous but formal font name Sabina or Sabyn. From *Sil* the surnames *Sibbet, Sibbons, Sibellas* and *Sibson* originate. *Sibbald,* and *Sibary* are from the Teutonic *Sigebeald*.

Matilda, that stately name borne by several Norman ladies of royal blood has also the pet forms *Maud, Maw* and sometimes *Malkyn,* and these in their turn survive in the surnames *Maudson, Mawson, Makins* and *Makinson.* The last two are also from Matthew.

From *Bab,* the shortened form of Barbara, come the surnames *Babb, Babbs, Babcock, Barbotte.*

In Burke's *Landed Gentry* (edition 1849) occurs an explanation of the origin of the Scottish surname Majoribanks that may be read in connection with the preceding paragraph on the baptismal name Margaret.

" When Walter, High Steward of Scotland, and ancestor of the royal house of Stewart married Marjorie (Margaret) only daughter of Robert Bruce, the barony of Ratho was granted by the King as a marriage portion to his daughter, by a charter which is still extant ; and these lands being subsequently denominated *Terra de Ratho Margorie-banks*. This gave rise to the surname Majoribanks."

CHAPTER VII

Names from Miracle Plays

> HAMLET : " Good my lord, will you see the players
> well bestowed ? Do you hear, let them be well used,
> for they are the abstract and brief chronicles of the
> time : after your death you were better have a bad
> epitaph than their ill-report while you live."—
>
> *Hamlet*, Act II, Sc. ii.

SOME fifty or sixty years ago it was generally agreed
by those who built ingenious theories to account for
surnames, that those who bore the names *King, Prince,
Duke, Earl, Abbot*, received them through ancestors
who had been servants of these august personages.   It
was also further explained that as kings and princes
have always more servants than their followers the
swelling numbers of kings and princes in the Directories
were easily accounted for.

But this theory did not account for the *Postles*
(apostles), *Martyrs, Sowdens* (Sultans), the *Fryers*
(friars) or the *Ankrett* (anchorite).   Indeed, it is nothing
more than a finely spun cob-web of fancy, and like
many other theories of expounders who tried to settle
philological problems by airy flights of imagination,
it disappeared.

The Mediæval peasant looked to the Church for
his amusements and recreations, and the churchyard
was his playground.   There he gambled, diced, carried

on cock-fights, played the quarter-staff and danced. At Christmas he drank Church ale there and generously paid for the liquor, made from his own malt and barley.

But the Church had better fare to offer than this. Knowing that the love of the symbol is innate in human nature, the ecclesiastical authorities introduced liturgical drama into the Church services at Easter. Simple this was and crude but it appealed to people of all nationalities. Following this came the Nativity Play and The Play of the Three Kings, which were parts of the Christmas ceremony in the Church. In the fulness of time the Miracle Play gained amazing popularity and infinitely greater than that " attained by any other form of drama before or since," as Mr. E. Hamilton Moore reminds us in his careful study of the *English Miracle Plays and Moralities.*

Like so many other institutions the Drama came into this country with the Normans. But soon Rome became suspicious of the miracle play in which many indecorous impromptus had been introduced, and the clergy were forbidden to take part in them. But at the same time religious plays were associated with the feast of Corpus Christi.

Freed from the trammels of the Church the Miracle Play began to pulse with new life. The characters even when they represented patriarch or prophet spoke in the broad vernacular and infused the parts with homely vigour and native wit. So was born the English Drama. Chaucer's " Wife of Bath " was one of the immense multitude that travelled to the towns where the finest performances of the Corpus Christi plays were to be seen. On these occasions a cycle of plays forming a sequence from the " Creation of the World " to the " Day of Judgment " were acted.

In 1397 Richard II went to York to witness the performances there. At York as elsewhere the plays were acted on movable stages called Pageants, and these succeeded each other at various stations in the city.

In all towns and villages Mystery plays were performed and for more than three centuries the Drama was the instructor of the people in matters of faith and morals. It was also the most popular form of recreation and it was one that was free to all. The poorest of the poor could enjoy it. Instead of waiting for an audience within the four walls of a theatre, as they do today, the players took out their movable pageant into the highways, wheeled it to the cross-roads where the crowd awaited them, and there gave their performances. When they had finished there, they moved on to another station and acted another play. A special Guild was formed whose duty it was to arrange and perform these plays, but in the large towns, notably at York, Chester and Coventry, all the members of all the craft Guilds took part in them.

Nor were these entertainments confined to the common people. Royalty as we have seen patronised the play and whenever the King travelled through the shires, plays and interludes were arranged for his amusement in the castles and mansions where he stayed. The chief duty of noblemen's chaplains was to prepare plays for the private chapels under their charge a

Christmas and Easter. The Household Accounts of
the Earl of Northumberland (1512-1525) make mention
of these plays, and the fees that were to be paid to
the players :

" If my Lord's chaplain be a maker of Interludes he
is to have a servant for writing out the parts, else none
. . . My Lord useth and accustometh to give them
of his chapel if they do play the Play of the Nativity
upon Christmas Day, twenty shillings . . . To
pay for rewards to players for plays played at Christmas
by *strangers* in my house, twenty pence every play."

These *strangers* were not strolling players, as we shall
presently see, but competent and experienced actors
to whom alone the acting of mystery plays was
entrusted.

The Miracle play which began as a Church monopoly
became, as we have seen, a national institution. The
Church held its high festivals in which processions were
a conspicuous feature but except at the festival of
Corpus Christi, it had no interest nor took any part in
the Miracle Play.

But towards the close of the sixteenth century the
Miracle Play had run its course. The Puritan hating
everything savouring of pleasure suppressed it. The
last performance of the cycle of plays in York was
given in 1584, just four years before Shakespeare wrote
" Love's Labour Lost." Coventry held out a few years
longer, but at last the people of that ancient town
realised the truth of the couplet set in the mouth of
one of the characters of the Protestant Morality Play,
" New Custom " :

Since these Genevan doctors came so fast into this land,
Since that time it was never merry with England.

At a meeting of the City Council held May 19th, 1591,
it was unanimously agreed : " That the *Destruction of
Jerusalem*, and either the *Conquest of the Danes*, or the
History of King Edward the Confessor, at request of the
Commons of this city, shall be played on pageants on
Mid-summer day and St. Peter's day in this city, and
none other plays : and all the maypoles that now are
standing in this city shall be taken down before
Whitsun Day next, and none hereafter to be put up in
this city."

So with the coming of Puritanism vanished the
maypole and the plays, and for seventy years thereafter
" the bigots of the iron-time " held sway in England,
but they were powerless to suppress, as they would
have liked, the dramatists, Shakespeare, Marlowe,
Ben Jonson, and others who amid much discourage-
ment evolved a drama wider in scope and richer in
poetic fancy and imagination than the world has
known, before or since.

The accounts of the Trade Guilds give information
as to the properties and costumes worn at the performances of the miracle.   The money spent on the stage
furniture suggests that the Treasurers of Guilds had
" frugal minds."   Thus we find that *Crowe*, probably
the local carpenter was paid 2s. for making three worlds,
which at eight pence apiece seems reasonable.   Then
there are items, " Paid for settynge the world of fyer,
five pence.   Item payd for kepying of fyer at hell-
mouth, fourpence.   Item payd for starche to make the

storme in the Pagents, sixpence." A barrel was used for producing an earthquake and a real rope for Judas.

The most fearsome and popular of all characters was the Devil. In *Gammer Gurton's Hodge*, this forerunner of the modern Harlequin had " Horns to push, as long as your two arms, with a long cow's tail, and crooked cloven feet, and many a long nail. He wore a horrible looking mask and carried a cudgel, and with this he struck at all within reach.

The greatest care was taken in the selection of suitable actors for the different parts, and once a player had satisfied the Guild of his competence in a particular part he played it year after year. In some cases we find Guilds craving exemption from playing on account of their long service.

The actors were well paid for their work and were remunerated for the rehearsals as well as public performances. In the accounts we find " Item, payd to the demon, 1s. 4d. ; to Pilate his wyfe, 2s. ; to Fauston for cock crowing, three pence ; Item payd to two wormes of conscience, 1s. 4d. ; payd for a quart red wyn for Pilat, two pence ; and payd for o'r supper on the play day, for o'rselves, goodman Mawpas, the minstrell, the dresser of the Pagent, and the Gouvnor and his wyfe 4s."

We cannot wonder that the men who took the part of the knight or squire, shepherd or king, were accosted by their friends and acquaintances, first in jest, and afterwards when the reason for so calling them was forgotten, by the name they bore. In the present day the actor who is cast for the villain's part in transpontine

melodrama, is generally vigorously hooted, and sometimes assaulted by auditors who fail to distinguish the
actor from the man himself.   So it was in those past
centuries.   The man who played the high priest or the
tormentor, was priest or tormentor to those he knew.
If the name did not please him he looked out for a
favourable opportunity for changing it ; and either he
or his immediate descendants succeeded in doing this.

There is plenty of evidence in old records in support
of the assumption.   For in them we find such names as
Hamond le *King* and Reginald *Kyngesone* in the
Hundred Rolls ; Geoffrey le *Legat* (Legate) and
Thomas *Preist* in the same document ; Jeffrey *Prince*
(Cal. Proceedings in Chancery, Elizabeth) ; Hugh le
Pope and Alan le *Pope* (Hundred Rolls) ; Walter
Cardinal (Issue Rolls) ; John le *Bissup* (Bishop) and
Walter *Pilate* (Hundred Rolls).   There are many more.
Some have become obsolete ; others have taken on
strange forms through dialectical pronunciation and
eccentric spelling.   But an examination of the dramatis
personæ of some of the old plays explains many entries
in the old rolls that could not otherwise be accounted
for.

On this subject of names from the Miracle Plays,
Camden speaks with special authority because not only
was he a distinguished antiquarian but he was also
Ben Jonson's teacher at Westminster School, and in
after years enjoyed his close friendship.   It is possible,
therefore, that he was also personally acquainted with
Shakespeare and other members of that brilliant
company that gathered at the Mermaid Inn.   His view

then on this point is entitled to attention. He says :

" Names also have been taken of civil honours, dignities and estate, as King, Duke, Prince, Lord, Baron, Knight, Valvasor or Vavasor, Squire, Castellan, partly for that their ancestours were such, served such, acted such parts ; or were Kings of the Bean."

All these character names form one of the multi-tudinous groups of nick surnames, to which reference will be made in further chapters.

King and *Prince* are both common surnames. *Prest*, *Press*, *Fryer* and *Frere* represent the lower clergy in the surname roll. The legate appears in Directories as *Leggatt*. The *croysyer* of olden times, whose duty it was to carry the cross, is represented by the modern *Crozier*. The names *Pope, Pontifix, Cayzer*, and its later form *Cæsar, Barron, Duke, Earl* and *Lord* are high sounding names borne by many who make no undue claims on our respect. *Duke* or *dux* often meant the leader in any enterprise or movement. In old records the name is entered as *Dook* and *Duke*, and the latter name appears in the Hundred Rolls. The early form *Keser* has blossomed into *Cayzer, Kaiser* and *Keyser* as well as the Cayzers and Cæsars already mentioned. To the school-boy of mid-Victorian days *Julius Cæsar*, the famous professional cricketer, was a much more attractive figure than his earlier namesake who conquered Gaul and Britain. In one of the Nativity plays, one of the Magi says :

> Certain Balaam speakys of this thyng
> That of Jacob a star shall spryng
> That shall overcom *Kasar* and Kyng.

Langland also uses the name in a notable passage :

> " Death cam dryvynge after,
> And al to duste passed
> Kynges and Knyghtes
> Kaysers and popes
> Lered and lewed " (Learned and ignorant).

A compound of King may be seen in the Hundred Rolls as Will *Letleking*.

The Biblical names so prominent in these early plays, like those of Adam, Abel, Cain, Abraham, Isaac, Jacob, Joseph, David, those of the prophets, evangelists and disciples have already been dealt with in another chapter, but there are others to which reference must be made.

The surname Pagan was common in early records, and we find the names *Pagan a la Legh* and Roger filius *Pagan* in the Hundred Rolls. Some writers say they have been unable to find the name among modern Directories, but there are quite a number of families bearing the name *Pagan* in Cumberland, and the author was personally acquainted with a tradesman who owned it. The Painer or Tormentor who imparted realism to the old drama by zealously stoking up the fires of Hell and performing other grisly deeds still lives among surnames as *Poyner* and *Poynor*.

The minstrel was indispensable at these Pageants, and his former name Minstrell along with that of *Organer* appears in ancient documents. The *Wait* which means primarily a watchman was also used for these instrumentalists. But this name has also another origin and is a nickname for a grower of wheat. The

Bannerman, who walked alone between the crafts in the Corpus Christi processions was an official of importance, and carried out duties similar to those of the modern advertising man.   As Mr. A. W. Pollard says in the Introduction to his *English Miracle Plays :*

" Its performance (the Croxton play) though localised at Croxton, whether permanently or not we cannot say, was announced throughout the neighbouring villages by *venillatores* or banner-bearers, of the same kind as those who advertised the plays of the itinerant actors who represented the ' Coventry ' cycle and the *Castell of Perseverance.*"

The surname *Banner* is found in various parts of England, but *Bannerman* is mostly found across the border.   The Latinised form of the latter word, *pennager*, has yielded the surnames *Penniger* and *Pennigar*, *Pinegar* and *Pinnegar*.   The judge as pronouncer of doom " le Demester," from which comes the name *Dempster*.   The *Deemster* is still a judge's title in the Isle of Man.   By epenthesis *armiger* the Latin for esquire becomes *Arminger* in the modern surname, and the same change occurs in *claviger*, macebearer, which is now *Clavinger*.

Virgin is rare as a surname, but the Latin equivalents *Virgo* and *Virgoe* are frequently met with.

The name of the Deity obviously borne by a Pageant performer is found in the Hundred Rolls as *Hugh Godde*.   In the Writs of Parliament the name *Roger Godde* appears.   The modern surname version is *Good*, which is well represented in the Directories.   It is also the first element in many compounds.

The Miracle Plays furnished rich and ample material for those who wished to exercise their wit and ingenuity by giving their friends names that would stick. The name Bishop was first conferred in the thirteenth century. We find it in the Hundred Rolls as John le *Bissup* and the Patent Calend. as Robert le Biscop. Two hundred years later the name had become *Byshoppe*. Today the numbers of those bearing this and other high sounding names remind us of those halcyon days depicted by W. S. Gilbert when " Dukes were three a penny," and

> Party leaders you might meet
> By twos and threes in every street
> Discussing with no little heat
> Their various opinions.

In the old Nativity plays the shepherds appear in strong force and have leading parts. As the names of characters in the cast are given in Latin, each one is called *Pastor*. But to the populace he was known by the English name, and so in the Hundred Rolls we have Josse le *Sephurde*, and in the Writs of Parliament John le *Shepherde*. But this was not only a nickname. It also designated the owner's occupation.

Angels had also leading parts in these days and from the players of these the names *Angel*, *Angelis*, *Angell* and *Angelo* descend.

The *Pilgrim*, *Prophete*, *Monck* and *Seynt* of the old records were also represented in the Pageants. Since then they have figured in the surname list, with some slight alteration in spelling as *Pilgrim*, *Prophet*, *Monk* and *Saint*.

Even the grim figure of Death that struck terror into the hearts of the audiences that witnessed these plays imposed on the hapless actor who performed the part this surname of ill-omen. In the Writs of Parliament and the Hundred Rolls appear the names John *Deth* and Hugh de *Dethe*, the forerunner of the *Deaths* of modern Directories.

A notable feature of the Miracle and Mystery plays to which Mr. A. W. Pollard draws attention is, that the characters with whom the medieval dramatist felt himself free to deal, are " almost exclusively those of persons to whom neither Scripture nor legend ascribed either name or individuality. Cain's Garcio or servant, Noah's wife, the Detractors of the Blessed Virgin, the shepherds, the soldiers sent to slay the Holy Innocents, the Pharisees who brought before Christ the woman taken in adultery . . . it is in the treatment of these nameless characters that some of the most dramatic touches are bestowed."

In one of the York plays the subject of which is the Crucifixion, Pilate, who is waiting the arrival of Jesus, shows his affection for his wife in a manner unbefitting his dignity, and for this he is reproved by his Beadle. But beadle is much older than the Miracle plays, and is from Anglo-Saxon *bytel*, M. English bidden, to ask, pray. And it is also from Old French *Bedel*. From these we have several surnames. Godwin *Bedellno* is written in *Domesday Book*. The modern variants of the name are *Biddle*, *Beadell*, *Beadle*, *Buddle*, *Beaddall*.

There can be little doubt that in most instances

these names are taken from the offices held by their original owners, but it may be assumed as well, that at times they are nicknames, and that the player who took the leading part in so remarkable an incident was nicknamed the *Beadle* by his friends and neighbours.

The parable of Dives and Lazarus was a favourite theme with the authors of old plays, and in one of the most dramatic of these Lazarus is introduced as the son of King Cyrus, and becomes Lord of Jerusalem. As brother of Mary Magdalen the " heroine " of the play he vainly endeavours to protect her from the machinations of Satan and his legions. A player of such prominence could scarcely hope to escape the attention of the wits in his audience, and it is not surprising to find his name, together with that of Elyas le *Dives* in the thirteenth century records. The prevalence of the name Lazarus at the present day, is partly due to the immigration of foreign Jews.

The unbelievers who were so mercilessly lectured by those animated shades—Justice, Mercy, Contemplation, Truth and others, were generally represented by Saracen, Heathen, Hatechrist and Shunchrist. Peter *Sarracen* and Walter *Sarazein* are both to be found in the Patent Rolls. Nicholas fil *Sarre* appears in the Hundred Rolls. The modern representatives of these are *Sarasin* and *Sarson*. Walter de *Hethen's* name is in the Patent Rolls, but this surname is now possibly extinct. The same fate has probably overtaken *Hatewrong* and *Hatechrist* which figure so prominently in the old dramatic homilies, and are represented as well in early records. But on this point it is impossible to speak positively as surnames have a curious trick of cropping up in the most unexpected places. The name Shonecrist (Shunchrist), the type of name Bunyan used in his immortal allegories, may be found in the Hundred Rolls. As the first holder of this name probably represented the stiff-necked and unrepentant in the old moralities, it is impossible not to feel a little sympathy for him as he listened meekly to wearisome exhortations and lurid predictions of the punishments that lay in store for him. When we consider these and other curious surnames our wonder is, not that they have become obsolete, but that so many of them held their ground so long, and outlived many generations.

The name *Proud* is in the Hundred Rolls, and *Pride* in Fine Rolls, and we discover, too, *Proudfoot*, *Proudman* and *Proudlove*. In contrast with these there are also *Upright* (Riley's *Memorials of London*). We still have our Uprights—by name at least, and according to Bardsley, a person of this name appeared at a trial at Exeter in October, 1874.

A clergyman bore the more or less appropriate name of *Ryghtwys* (Righteous) and was Vicar of Foulden in Norfolk in 1497 (Bromefield's *Norfolk*). This is also a pageant name. *Patience* still survives as a surname, as do *Wise, Best, Merry, Merriman* (William Merry-man—Valor Ecclesiasticus). A member of the present House of Commons is distinguished from his fellow members by the surname *Wise*, and a distinguished journalist recently deceased was named *Le Sage*. We find his namesake Geoffrey *le Sage* in the Fine Rolls. *Best* is a name of respectability, for in the Hundred

Rolls it appears as Richard le *Beste*, and it is also found in other records. In contrast to these the name Walter *Fulhardy* (*Foolhardy*) is quoted by Riley in his *Memorials of London*.

Mr. Lower discovered a Maud *Make-Joy* in an old Wardrobe Account, December 26th, 1297, while in two separate rolls appear the names Julian *Make-bliss* and John *Make-blythe*. The Maud Make-joy just mentioned, true to her name, was honoured by a royal command, and danced before Edward, Prince of Wales, at Ipswich, for which she received as remuneration 2s.

The names William le *Lewed* (Lewd) and John le *Luwed* were common six hundred years ago, but they have long since become obsolete. But in early days the name had not the sinister meaning that it has now. It meant ignorant or unlearned, and the lewd-man was what the " layman " is now.

Thus in the *Secunda Pastorum* of the Towneley Plays the Third Shepherd says :

> I am redy and yare : go we in fere
>   To that bright
> Lord, if thi wylles be,
> We are *lewde* alle thre
> Thou grauntt us soinkyns gle (Joy)
> To comforth thi wight.

The adjectives *Gay*, *Blithe*, *True* and *Leal* are all found as early surnames, and as they are complimentary they have suffered no change with the lapse of time. *Giddyhead* (William Gidyheved), Glutton (Gilbert Glutun)—the latter of these appears in the Calend. Genealogicum—have naturally passed away, and left no modern successors.

Warin Cruel may have been fiercely proud of the surname that stamped him as a man of character, but his successors—if he had any—had other views, and the name is but a relic of a long forgotten past. In the same record we find Ralph le Fere (*Fierce*), William le Wilfulle (*Wilful*), Hamo le Enveyse (*Envious*). These uncomplimentary names have also disappeared from Burgess Roll and Directory. To these may be added the name *Sullen*, which has its place in the ancient rolls.

Against these we have a number of adjectival surnames indicating more commendable qualities, but which like the others spring from the love of the medieval peasant for pageant and procession.

The first of these is *Hardy*, a name that has been made illustrious by more than one of its bearers. In the Hundred Rolls the name appears as *Hardi ;* in the Writs of Parliament it is spelt as today with a final *y*.

True is not only a complimentary surname, but it also appears in several compounds, so that we have Trewbody (*Truebody*), Trewlove (*Truelove*) and Treueman (*Truman*). Stephen Trewbody has a place in the Rolls of Parliament. So has Stephen Truelove, while in the Hundred Rolls we find Agnes Treueman and Thomas Treweman. All these names have their modern representatives.

Kind and *Kindness* are both found in the ancient Rolls.

The name *Virtue* has many representatives in our present day Directories, many more indeed than it had when the old Rolls were compiled. *Vice* also is a flourishing surname. But there was much confusion in the Middle Ages and later as to the precise meaning attached to the terms in the early plays. On this matter Mr. A. W. Pollard speaks with unequalled authority :

" An example of this confusion is to be found in the prominence assigned in all accounts of the Morality to the character of Vice, to whom allusion is made by Ben Jonson in his *Staple of News*, II, 1, and *The Devil is an Ass*, I, 1, and by other Elizabethan writers. In the Morality proper the Vice has no part, but when the desire was felt for some humorous relief in the didactic interludes, a character probably dressed in the traditional garb of the domestic fool was introduced and attained great popularity. The etymology of the name is doubtful, for in Heywood's *Play of the Wether* (1534) one of the earliest instances in which the Vice is specifically mentioned by name, he plays the part of *Mery Report*, who is a jester pure and simple, without any connection with any of the deadly sins. So in *Jack Juggler*, Jack himself is called the *Vice* and in *Godly Queen Hester* (1561) the name is given to a jester called *Herdy Derdy*. In other plays, however, the part of the Vice is assigned to characters such as *Sin, Fraud, Inclination, Ambition*, etc., and the list given in *The Devil is an Ass* (Fraud or Covetousness or lady Vanity or old Iniquity) confirms the theory that the obvious etymology is the true one."

So the plays by which our surname lists have been so greatly enriched at last ran their course. They were crude in form and almost destitute of the qualities of imagination and poetic feeling that give distinction to great drama. But it was the drama of the uncultured who strove in vain to break the narrow bonds of a convention which authority imposed on this form of art. But the plays were not dull and didactic enough for the Puritans who suppressed them. Yet whatever their defects these old Miracle and Mystery plays fulfilled a great purpose. They unfolded before the eyes of these simple and unlettered people a new world of thought and ideas. These they saw at first as through a glass darkly. But afterwards they were able to distinguish their surroundings more clearly, and they grew in mental and moral stature. It would be foolish and unjust to judge these plays by modern standards. Their authors were feeling their way to a new form of expression, and they had no examples to guide them, for as yet the Greek Drama was practically unknown in England. The tiny stage was little more than an enlarged box, and on this there was little room for action. This difficulty was met in different ways. In the stage directions we are told " Herod rages in the street and on the stage." But the interest was principally sustained by long speeches in which the story of the play was unfolded.

The time had come for ringing down the curtain. The old play was dead and the age that gave it birth had vanished into the twilight of history, and with it had passed the Medieval peasant, with his child-like gaiety and irresponsible humour. The Englishman who took his place breathed an ampler air. Freed from the Feudal and Ecclesiastical domination that had oppressed his ancestors, he accepted with joy the treasures that Fortune with lavish hand poured into his lap—the printing press, the grammar school, and universities revitalised by the Renaissance.   England's wealth and power were growing apace, and every year seamen brought wondrous stories of newly discovered countries and their marvellous store of gold and gems. Then a strange young man had come to London from Warwickshire who at his grammar school at Stratford-on-Avon had probably conned the texts of the old moralities, and at the feast of Corpus Christi had watched the Coventry pageant and seen Herod rage, and beheld the fearsome spectacle of the Devil with horns and tail, and the sight had given him food for thought.   To this favourite of the Muses was entrusted the task of shaping a new Drama, a Drama that was to become the wonder and admiration of mankind.

But let us think kindly of the old Miracle plays to which we owe so much, and from which even Shakespeare himself borrowed ideas.   And not the least part of our debt are the surnames they bequeathed to us. From these we gather what may be considered trifles— shreds and patches of information, but which when compared, classified and pieced together add not a little to our knowledge of those by-gone centuries, and help us to understand more clearly the thoughts, actions and speech of the early fathers of our race.

CHAPTER VIII

Fourteenth Century London

THE ancient documents preserved in the Archives of the City of London Guildhall are priceless bequests from early City Fathers to their successors. They form an almost unbroken record of City life for more than six hundred years. Apart from the Royal Charters that secure the liberties of the citizens, the Pleas and Memoranda Rolls, the Inquest Rolls, and the Letter Books provide the student with an almost inexhaustible mine of historical information. These musty parchments unfold for those that care to read the multicoloured pageant of London life through the passing centuries. As they read, those with imagination and sympathy can people again the narrow crooked streets and see the dignified city merchant in his furs, the richly clad Abbot, the craftsman in his livery, the hucksters and piemen shouting their wares, the lackpennys and outcasts gazing greedily at the provisions piled on the street booths. But in addition to conjuring up these pictures these Rolls describe with great wealth of detail the strenuous exertions of the Mayor and Corporation to enforce order and discipline on a turbulent and unruly population. We see them, too, taking counsel with the King on high matters of

State, supplying him with money and provisions, fortifying the city against foreign invaders, and administering stern and generally even-handed justice.

The accounts we get in these Rolls are of a life which while resembling our own in some points, is yet strangely different, and it is this difference that piques our curiosity and invests the record with perennial interest and fascination.

In names alone a slow and silent revolution had been effected in the two previous centuries, but they were not yet stabilised. Many of them were much different in form from their modern counterparts. In some cases people were known by more than one surname. Thus in the Calen. of Letter Book H. we read that " John *Tykhill* ' bochier,' otherwise called John *Skyft*, and others have been maintainers of plaints." In the same record the name of a surety in a case of guardianship is given as William *Kelshulle*, otherwise called *Convers*, fishmonger.

In many examples the font and surnames were still separated by *atte* or *de* or *le* as in *atte Cellar*, *atte Lathe*, *atte Pond*, *atte Milne* and *atte Conduit*, this last being the name of a Mayor of the City.

The medieval *Cellar* has in our time become *Sellar* and *Sellars*, by a change of the initial consonant. *Lathe* appears to be obsolete. *Pond* and *Milne* are still flourishing surnames. The name *Conduit* though by no means common, still survives in its original form.

Among the various classes the local names of origin vastly preponderate. Many are in the old forms and the definite article or a preposition precedes the

surname, as in *Thomas le Northerne, Gilbert de Notyng-
ham, John de Kirketon, Thomas of Newcastle.* But in
the later lists of the fourteenth century there are signs
of change in the direction of simplification, and in
several of the local names the particle is omitted, as in
John Grantham, John Hanampsted or *Hampsted.* But
at this period these shortened names were exceptional.

Thus in January, 1365, we find that *Roger atte Grene*
was committed to prison for rebellious conduct towards
the masters of the mistery of Cordwainers, and that
Adam de Lynne suffered the same fate for using bad
language in contempt of the King and his court.

Henry de Newport, fishmonger, was committed to
prison for using unseemly and horrible words (*verba
inonestia et orribilia*) to *Robert atte Noke* (R. at the oak),
chandler, in court.

Richard de Berdefeld, rector of the Church of
Wolchurchehawe was mainprised to keep the peace
with John *Courdi (Courey).*

John atte Ree and *Robert de Berkyng,* beadle, entered
into a bond in £40 that " the said John would cease
playing with false dice."

We also find several derivatives from the word *cot*
among the surnames in these Rolls. This word has
more than one meaning. In the forms *cott* and *cot* it is
used in Ireland for a little boat, and many places in
that country derive their names from it. (See Joyce's
Irish Names of Places, I, 226.) The word is used in
this sense by Spenser in his *Faerie Queen.* It is
derived from the Irish *coit, coite,* a small boat.

The peasant's hut was also known as a *cot* or *cote,*

and its master the *Cotter*. *Cot-queen* as used by the
Elizabethan dramatists connoted a " scold," or a man
who did woman's work. From *cot* spring the surnames
Coates, *Cotman* and *Cotteril*. It is also an element in
many compound surnames, e.g. *Caldecott*, *Estcote*,
Westcott, *Northcote*, *Southcott*.

In a long list of names of people convicted of
immorality, the majority of whom were chantry priests,
appears the name of Lawrence *Caldecote*.

Local names in which the preposition before the name
has survived and become part of it may be found in
Bythewater and *John-in-the-Lane*. *Bythewater* appears
frequently in the City Rolls as the name of an influential
Alderman. *John in the Lane* was an apprentice to
Richard atte Well, goldsmith, who took an oath that he
would teach his prentice the trade, and not send him
into the country to thresh his corn.

Bythewater has long since been shortened to *Bywater*
and *Byewater*, though the name *Bytheway* still exists
as a rather rare surname, together with *Byway*.
Modern directories also have *Bysouth*, *Byham*, *Bygrave*,
Byford, *Bylock*, *Bycroft*. With these may be compared
John Binethinthetowne which appears in the Patent
Rolls. When it dropped its connecting links *Lane*
became one of the commonest of surnames. *Atte Well*,
as mentioned in another chapter, has developed into
the surnames *Wells* and *Attwell*.

Again we find that *William Moot*, brewer, was
concerned in an affray in Candlewick Street. William's
conduct, which was doubtless shocking, does not
concern us here, but his name presents an interesting

problem. *Moot* has alternative origins. It may be, and probably is, in some examples a local name, and stands for *moat*, or one of those trench defences the Normans constructed in sodden ground. On the other hand it may, like *Mott*, be a diminutive form of *Matilda*.

Turning to patronymics, an entry of October, 1381, informs us that John Abbot was charged with abusing the King and all those who had caused men to be hanged in the recent Rebellion. *Abbot* may sometimes be a nickname given to a pageant player, but it also is one of the many derivatives of Abraham or Abel.

An interesting name in the Rolls is that of *Hugh Alwyne*, tiler. This is a Norman French adaptation of the Anglo-Saxon *Ælfwine* (fairy, friend). Its modern forms are *Alwin, Alwyn, Alwyne, Elvy, Elvey, Elvin* and *Elwin*.

The name *Alryht* represented in the Rolls by one *Hugh* is also of Anglo-Saxon descent and is a corruption of *Ealdric*, of which the suffix *ric* means powerful.

We meet also that once popular name *Amelryk*, borne by a Bruges merchant of whom it is recorded that he sent a Letter of Attorney to a London citizen. A metathesis of this name Almaric is famous in epic story. Like so many other names of Teutonic origin which represent abstract ideas *Amalric* is from *Amal*, meaning work. One of its many derivatives is *Amory* which appears in the City Rolls as *Ammory*.

Bardsley is scarcely correct in saying that the patronymic surnames *Andrew* and *Anderson* nearly all belong to the north side of the Tweed, for in the City Rolls we find *Andrew* represented by goldsmiths, poulterers, brewers and drapers, while one James *Andrew* was Mayor in 1367-8.

Adam was then, as now, a favourite surname, and its derivatives *Ade* and *Adys* are also represented.

Aubrey, with several representatives in these Rolls, is from the name *Alberic* introduced by the French, and adopted by them from Teutonic sources.

The common patronymics all find places in these rolls—*Hervy, George, Jacob, James, Johan, Jonneson, Josepe, Joskyn, Lucas, Luke, Mark, Martin, Mathen, Gibbs, Gilbert, Mychell* (Mitchell), *Percival, Phelip, Simon, Symcok, Olyver, Symme, William, Dawe, Davy Danyel* and many more. Surnames with the prefix *Fitz* are also common and among these may be found *Fitz Alan, Fitz Andrew, Fitzhugh, Fitz John, Fitz Mary* (Sheriff of London), *Fitznicholl, Fitz Roger, Fitzsimond, Fitz Thomas, Fitz Walter* and *Fitz Piers*.

Names that indicate occupations or office are of great interest because they disclose a social and industrial organisation so different from that of the present day. Many of the surnames in these Rolls give the names of crafts and trades that disappeared ages ago, yet in several instances the names that point to these occupations still survive.

In the fourteenth century the craft of the armourer was one of national importance. The *mistery* of Armourers in London sent two members to the Common Council. But the scientific development of firearms killed the armourer's craft. Yet the name survives like several other occupational names, without the agential suffix. Thus Michael *Armourer* who lived in the reign of

9

Edward III has since become *Armour*, just as treasurer
leaves the surname *Tressure*, and *Spicerer*, *Spicer*.

Of names of office we find Roger *Shirreve*, John le
Coroner, William le *Buteler*, Edmund *Chamberleyn*, John
Marchal, John *Squier*, Thomas *Serjaunt*, John *Reve*,
John *Usher*.

At the time the entries were made in the Rolls these
names must have been long fixed, for very few of those
bearing them have the same profession or trade.   Thus
we find that the John *Coroner* whose name appears in
1375 is a fishmonger, Edmund *Chamberleyn*, a glover,
F. *Serjeunt*, a skinner, and John *Usher*, the City
Chamberlain.   John *Smyth* was the City Saltmeter,
Thomas of the same name was City Cornmeter, John
Brewer was a carter, and Nicholas *Bocher* bailiff of
Southwark, and John *Baker* a brewer.

Entries in the Rolls in which bearers of occupative
names figure are many and illuminating.   Several of
them are of trades like those of Taverners and
Chaundlers, that in these days would not be regarded
as " misteries."

Thus one entry states that Bartholomew le *Furner*
(a baker's oven man) was committed to prison for
contempt and trespass against the assayers of white
bread.   His employer and other guarantors undertook,
" body for body, that no damage or peril should befall
the said assayers."

" John Bernes, *altakere* of the King came into court
and paid Simon *Brewere* the sum of 100 shillings and
20 pence for ale taken for the King's use by tally and
without tally."

The most illustrious among these occupative names is that of Geoffrey *Chaucer*. There are three entries in the City Rolls which have been reprinted in the *Life Records of Chaucer*, but only the first of these makes a direct reference to him. It is as follows :

" Quit claim by Richard Goodchild, cutler, and John Grove, armourer, to Geoffrey Chaucer Esquire, of all actions demands, etc. Dated at London 28 June, 1380."

It is not possible to glean any knowledge of our first great poet, from the obscure reference to a financial transaction which this entry discloses, but the many allusions in the Calendar to Thomas Chaucer stir curiosity, and create an appetite for more. This curiosity has been satisfied, thanks to the investigations of Dr. Scott (late Keeper of the Manuscripts in the British Museum) who was eventually satisfied that Thomas Chaucer was the son of the poet. He was the King's chief butler, and as a Member of Parliament was five times elected Speaker of the House.

The surname *Chaucer* stands for *hosier* from Old French *chaussier*. The names John *Hosiere*, and John *Hosyer* also appear in the City Rolls, and others of this class are Philip *Draper*, Richard *Webbe*, weaver. To these should be added *Webbere*, *Webestre*, Adam *Litstere* and *Dyere*. *Litstere* from which we derive the modern *Lister* has the same meaning as Dyer and is from the M. English *litster*, a dyer. The Prompt. Parvulorm refers to the word as " *Lystare* or *Lytaster* of cloth diyynge—Tinctor." The same trade has also given us the surnames *Dyster* and *Dexter*.

The Mistery of Fullers has long since been swallowed up by the Clothworkers, but in the fourteenth century it was one of the most influential of the Guilds and sent no fewer than four members to the Common Council. In Newcastle-on-Tyne and other northern towns, companies of Fullers still exist, and one of the London City Churches is still known as St. Mary *Matfellon*. The *matfellon* was the fuller's *teazle* and one of the principal tools of the trade. The fuller's duty was to trample the cloth. The word is French in origin and is from the French *fouler*, to trample. Among the west of England clothmakers this work is known as tucking, and the craftsman there was known as a *Tucker*, which accounts for the popularity of this surname in that part of the country. In the northern centres where cloth is made the trampler of cloth is known as a *Walker*. In Wyclif's translation of the Bible, Mark ix. 3, the verse runs : " And his clothis ben maad schynynge and white ful moche as snow, and which maner clothis a *fullere*, or *walkere* of cloth may not make white on erthe."

In the City Rolls it is stated that Roger *Fuller* was summoned by the Mayor, along with other influential members of the Mistery, to assist in framing regulations for the control of the craft.

From the fuller's teasel comes the surname *Tozer*.

William *Chaloner* of the City Rolls was a cooper, but his name suggests quite a different occupation. For a chaloner was a dealer in *shallon*, known in earlier days as *chalon*, and this first form of the word indicates the place of origin of this commodity—

Chalons-sur-Marne. The Miller of Trumpington in Chaucer's *Reve's Tale*, who loved comfort

> In his owene chambre made a bedde
> With shetes and *chalons* fair yspredde.

The name survives as Challoner.

Associated with the trades already mentioned is *Tailleur* or *Taylleur* which we find well represented in the City Rolls. As the *Taylor* of modern times it is one of the most popular surnames. It has greatly added to its number by absorbing other names like *Teller* (weaver), and in some cases *Telfer* (French *Taillenfer*, cut-iron).

Though there were other names like *Parmenter* and *Seamer* for those who worked at this craft, it is unlikely that anyone belonging to the ancient and influential mistery of Tailors would assume any other surname.

The City has a peculiar affection for old custom, and has always jealously guarded its ancient privileges, and questions of precedence have led to more than one serious dispute between the City Companies. Precedence depended upon date of origin, but as it was uncertain as to when some of the charters were granted to the city companies, the Aldermen were confronted with the awkward problem of deciding the order in which the different Companies should march in procession. The Company most difficult to place in this matter was the Skinners. In 1339 they came to blows with the Fishmongers, and a hundred and fifty years later they had a long and heated wrangle with the Merchant Taylors on this question. It was then decided by the Lord Mayor, Robert Billesdon, that the

Skinners and Merchant Taylors should alternately take precedence of each other. This happy suggestion absolutely settled the dispute, and the arrangement made in that remote period has ever since been loyally carried out. The Merchant Taylors still give a dinner to the Skinners on St. John the Baptist's Day, a compliment which the Skinners afterwards return.

In the City Lists we find a John *Taillour*, as a juror in a case in which one Lawrence Newport was charged with forging a Papal Bull which he delivered to Robert *Herenvyt* (another occupative name), for a sum of ten marks; also of fraudulently obtaining another Bull called " cordery " from the house of the Abbot of Malmesbury. The prisoner was found guilty and condemned to the pillory. It may be noted that the term *cordery* had reference to an allowance of food or money, bestowed by a religious house. (See Calendar of Letter Books, Letter Book I, 105.)

Skynner was as well known as a surname in the Middle Ages as it is today. We find many *Skinners* in the City Rolls, and they are also well represented in other old records. In the Calendar of Inquests the name Richard le *Skynnere* appears, and in the Writs of Parliament Robert le *Skynnere*. We also discover the names *Tannur* and *Fellmonger*. *Currier* appears to belong to a later period.

We are told of one William *Skynnere* in the City Rolls who " entered into a bond of £10 to Richard *Palmere*, not to carry away the latter's wife again (*si plus caperet uxoreus suam in rapcionem*)."

Associated with the Skinners and Tanners in their trade were the *Barkers*, and their names appear as frequently as those of their associates. In the old Rolls we find such entries as *Barcur* and *Barkere*, as well as the Latinised *Barcarius*. In the City Rolls the name appears in the modern guise of *Barker*. The *Barker* family have added to their numbers by adopting the Anglo-French *berquier*, French *berger*, shepherd, to their numbers. In the conversation between King Edward IV and the Tanner of Tamworth town, as given in the popular ballad, published by Percy, we read :

> " What craftsman art thou ? " said the King ;
> " I pray thee telle me trowe,"
> " I am a Barker, Sir, by my trade ;
>   Now tell me, what art thou ? "

In the City records we read of a John *Barker*, underman, who was committed to prison on his confession that he served brewers for fourpence a day and his keep, and refused to be paid quarterly. This it may be explained was contrary to an ordinance of the City Authorities, forbidding payments by the day.

We find in the name *Pikeman* or *Pykeman* a reminder of a craft that has long become obsolete, like those of the *Spearman* and *Billman*.

The *Fourbour* did useful work in the armourer's workshop and scoured and polished the *habergeon* or coat of mail worn by the *Jackman*. Modern cavalry have superseded the Jackmen who fought England's battles in the Middle Ages, and the " jacks " or *habergeon* he wore now find a resting place in museums or the palatial mansions of American millionaires.

But we still retain the name in Directories and it serves to remind us of the fighting methods of ancestors whose bones have long since turned to dust. The *Fourbour* of the City Rolls and *le Fourbiours* of the Writs of Parliament have given way to our present day *Frobisher* and *Furbur*.

The maker of the *haubergeon*, the *hauberger*, was a common medieval name, but it is now very rare, if not altogether obsolete.

Those who bear the name of the greatest poet of antiquity may be interested to know that the surname comes from two sources, and one of these is the armourer's shop. For it is from Old French *heaumier*, helmet maker, and *Homer* is the popularly corrupted form of *le Heaumier*. The helmet was known either as the *healme* or *heaume*. In his *Richard III*, Hall thus speaks of the Battle of Bosworth Field :

" Lord, how hasteley the souldyoures buckled their healmes, how quickly the archers bent their bowes, and frushed their feathers, how redely the bilmen shoke their billes, and proved their staves."

Homer is also sometimes a local name of Teutonic origin and comes from *home* or *holm*, a river or lake island, as in *Lingholme* on Windermere and *Flatholme* in the Severn. *Stockholm* is on a river island.

Richard le *Kissere* mentioned by Riley in his *Memorials of London* may have practised the art of osculation as a pastime, but his working days were employed in making *cuishes* or armour to protect the thighs. In the careless barter of popular speech, the *cuicher*, as he was called soon became kisser, and this corruption of the term was embalmed in a surname that still survives.

The *Shether* made the slip that contained sword or knife. The word is from Icelandic *skeithir*, a sheath. From this branch of the armourer's trade we derive the *Sheather*. In the City Rolls it is recorded that Alice *Shether* was committed to prison as a common scold.

An interesting ceremony that in recent years has been allowed to lapse bears testimony to the symbolic significance which the sheath had in past times. Every year when a new Lord Mayor had been elected, the Corporation of the City visit the House of Lords to receive the Royal Assent to their choice. The Lord Chancellor, who receives them, announces the King's approval and according to ancient usage then drinks to the health of the Lord Mayor and Corporation in a loving-cup. The cup is then passed round, and the assembled officials follow his example. Then follows that part of the ceremony which has recently been discontinued. The city sword was borne into the presence of the Lord Chancellor. This was covered with a beautiful and elaborate scabbard of velvet. This scabbard was taken off by the Lord Chancellor and kept as a Royal perquisite, as an assertion of the Royal prerogative that the King alone can choose the time when the sword may be sheathed, and that for Royal protection it must ever be borne naked in the presence of the Sovereign.

As we are discussing swords it may be mentioned that in 1354 the City of London was granted the privilege of carrying its maces and swords upright, just as the State sword is carried before the King as a token of Sovereignty.

If we turn from the armourers to the Bowyers and the Fleechers we find quite a number of surnames awaiting us. At Cressy and Agincourt the English archers destroyed for ever the prestige of the man in armour, and in the fourteenth century the trades of making weapons of offence had became so important that the Bowyers and the Fleechers had become two separate " misteries." In making the bow and arrow there were several different crafts, the most important of which were those of the *Bowyer*, the *Fletcher*, and the *Stringer*. From the first we have the names, also *Boyer*, and sometimes *Bower*, for the latter is also a local name, as shown in another chapter. In addition to these there are *Arblast*, *Arblaster*, *Alabaster*, *Archer* and *Balaster*. *Bowman*, though sometimes a corruption of *Beaumont*, also generally belongs to the same group as also does *Bowmaker*.

In the City Rolls John *Bowyere* is mentioned as Keeper of the Bridge Gate, and William *Bowiere* as a Surveyor of the mistery of Skinners. According to the same records the latter was convicted of falsifying a deed enrolled in the Hustings, and was condemned to the pillory. An ordinance is also published in which citizens of London are warned to discontinue the practice of shooting arrows at the pigeons on Paul's Church.

We have already mentioned the fletcher or fledger whose duty it was to feather the arrow, but he was only one of the four craftsmen employed in making this important missile. Of these, the most responsible was the *arrowsmith* who made the head. That this work was not always done to the satisfaction of the authorities we learn from an Act of Parliament of 1405 in which the following ordinance is made : " Because the Arrowsmythe do make many faulty heads for arrows and quarels, it is ordained and established that all heads for arrows and quarels, after this time to be made, shall be well bolled or braised, and hardened at the points with steel."

To these craftsmen the *Arrowsmiths* owe their name. But, as is the way of Englishmen, the man in the street had other names for the arrowsmith and the arrow he flighted. For him the arrow was a *flo*, and its maker the *Floer* or *Flouer*. This name was soon adopted as a surname, and today as *Flower* and *Flowers* is popular and widespread.

Setters and the *Tippers* have also survived as surnames, though the trades they represent have long since disappeared.

As we are discussing armaments it may not be out of place to mention the *Slinger*, who, however, was not a craftsman but a soldier, and took his place with the pikemen and archers in the battles of the period. His name also finds its place among surnames.

As we might expect the purveying trades are well represented in the City Rolls, and prominent among these are the bakers. Perhaps the most curious of the surnames left us by this indispensable fraternity is that of Sara le *Bredmongestere* which is recorded in Riley's

Memorials of London. It need scarcely be said that this name is now obsolete. But there are several others that are still with us. Among them are *Baker*, *Bagster* or *Baxter*. The baking and brewing trades in the Middle Ages were mostly in the hands of women, and as *ster* was originally a feminine ending, the name *bakester*—the earlier form of *baxter*—reminds us of this fact. It is also highly probable that many of the French settlers in London were also engaged in this industry for in the *Valor Ecclesiasticus* and other old records, the name *Bulenger* from the French *Boulanger* occurs more than once. From this name we derive *Bullinger*, *Bollinger*, *Pollinger* and *Ballinger*. The *Furner* or oven man has already been mentioned. Enrolled among the *Pastelers* and *Pie-bakers* were the *pestours* and *pastemakers*, the names of whose occupations soon became surnames. It is probable that the successors of John le *Pastemakere* whose name appears in the Writs of Parliament, and others like him adopted other surnames, for it seems to have disappeared, but under the name *Pester* we still meet the successors of *Pesturs* and *Pestours* of ancient days.

In the City Rolls an ordinance is set out under April 23, 1383, that no huckster, cook, or piebakere "thenceforth buy ale to sell again, under penalty prescribed," nor sell any kind of fish or poultry, "before the hour of Prime, on pain of forfeiture."

This brings us to the consideration of *Cook*, one of the most popular of occupative names. Like *Smith* and *Wright* it is one of the few names of occupation to which *son* is added. As the names *Cookson*, *Smithson* and

Wrightson have flourished and multiplied, it seems a little strange that the filial desinence has not been added to more of the occupative names.

But Cook in early days assumed several forms, and some of these still exist. *Le Queux* is the French form of *Cook* and *Kew* is the modern form of *le Keu* which appears so frequently in the old records. *Henry le Cok* and *John Cook* of the City Rolls reappear with little change in our Directories as *Coke* and *Cook*.

The ordinances issued to Cooks and Bakers, as given in the City Rolls are interesting as showing the supervision by the Mayor and Corporation over the manufacture of this important article of food.

The *Pestour blank* (white-baker) was instructed to bolt his meal twice and use his diligence to make his servants work well in kneading. They were also to make four loaves for a penny. Furthermore no horse bread was to be made except of pure beans and peas without mixture of other grain or bran, under heavy penalties.

The different varieties of bread have furnished several surnames, and these take both English and French forms, at which we need feel no surprise as in London at least both languages were freely used.

Payn is generally a personal name and a shortened form of *Pagan*, but it is quite probable that it was sometimes conferred on bread-bakers as a sobriquet, and in time became a settled surname. For among compounds we find both *Wytebred* (now *Whitbred*) and *Whitebread*, together with *Blancpain* (Hundred Rolls) and *Blankpain* (City Rolls). This name still retains its vitality as *Blanchpain*.

In the City Records it is stated that on March 14, 1391, Isabella Lynchlade was charged with falsely accusing William Squier, chaplin, of having stolen a Bible, which the said William had purchased of the executors of Master William *Blankpayn*. She was found guilty and condemned to stand on " *le Thewe* " ordained for women for one hour. The name Matila *Havercake* (meaning Oatcake) appears in the Hundred Rolls, and is still to be found in parish lists in the north of England.

The Fishmongers were among the most active and influential trades in the early centuries but they have left a very small mark on the store of English surnames. In the City Rolls we find under an entry for April 17, 1368, the record of a bill of complaint by John *Fisshe* alleging that John Haliwell, his journeyman, had run off with his (the plaintiff's) wife Elizabeth, taking with him goods to the value of £200. The plaintiff was awarded 40 marks damages and the journeyman committed to prison.

We find also that *Robert Fissher* was sued for a small debt. Beside these names *Fisshe* and *Fissher* there are records of *Fisshwyf* and *Pesooner*, but the former of these is now obsolete, and *Pessoner* but rarely met with. The Scandinavian name for fish *Fisk*, has been more popular and is a well-known surname, and *Fishman* is not altogether uncommon. There is also a diminutive of *Fisk* in *Fiskin*. Richard le *Harenger* of the Hundred Rolls has found none to bear his name in modern times, nor has *Symon Haryngbredere* who figures in the same record.

We have alluded in the first chapter on Nicknames to the fact that the Englishmen of the early centuries were hard swearers, and it must now be recorded that they also enjoyed a Continental reputation as heavy drinkers. Their potations were deep and prolonged. Reginald Pecock, who was Bishop of Chichester in 1444, denounced the immoderate use of beer, from which as he said, " *so myche horrible synne cometh, myche more than of setting up of ymages or of pilgrymagis.*" But all to no purpose ; temperance was unknown, and drunkenness the vice of every class.

From this prosperous trade many surnames have come down to us. The City Rolls mention names like Robert *Vynour*, Richard *Vinter*, *Vine*, *Brewer*, *Breouse* or *Brewes*, *Brewster* and *Maltster*. Others of the early names are *Viners*, *Vineturs* and *Vineters*. *Beerbrewer* was then a common surname, but *Tapper* is rare. Bardsley mentions the name of Johannes *Mashemaker* who signed the ordinances of St. Edmund's Guild, Bishop's Lynn. The names *Vine*, *Viner* and *Viney* are still popular.

But these names do not exhaust the list. In the old Rolls we also meet the names *Braciator*, *Bracer* and la *Bracerosse*. These are all from the French *brasseur*, of which *Braciator* is the Latinised form. From this old name the present day *Brasher* has come down to us.

This prosperous trade has been controlled in the City of London for several centuries by that powerful Guild, the Vintners' Company. As long ago as the reign of Henry VII, a charter was granted to this Company by virtue of which any free Vintner might sell wine in the City, without paying licence to the excise authorities.

This charter was confirmed by Edward VI and Queen Elizabeth. Attempts have since been made to deprive the Company of this privilege, and some slight modification was made in 1829, but the definite commercial privilege still exists, and so long as the free Vintner does not " sanction or connive at any bawdry on the premises," and enforces " good honest conversation by the frequenters thereof," his house is free from licence.

In nothing is the difference between the fourteenth and the twentieth century shown more clearly than in the methods employed in dealing with ailments and diseases. In the Middle Ages and for long afterwards anyone suffering ill-health was left to the anything but tender mercies of Barber Surgeons, who had their mistery and were granted special privileges as some recompense for their responsible duties. But in London the authorities seem to have had some doubt of the surgical skill of the barbers for in May, 1455, Simon Rolf and Richard Wellys, were appointed Surveyors of those exercising the faculty of surgery in the City ; and two months later an ordinance was published forbidding barbers practising the faculty of surgery in the City, to tend serious cases of illness without showing the patients to the above Surveyors, under penalty of a fine.

In some provincial centres the Barber-Surgeon was also a grocer. In 1273 the Mayor of York was John le Espicer aut Apotecarius. Among the early names taken from this trade or profession are le *Surgien*, *Blodlettere*, *Potecary*, *Barbour* and *Barbars*. The Hundred Rolls has also *Matilda la Barbaresse* and *Isabelle le*

Barbaresse.   From this we discover that the lady barber is not a modern innovation, as some of our antifeminists have supposed.

Another name which became very popular and which has since retained its hold is that of *Leech* or *Leach*.   It has altered very little in form for in the early records it appeared as *le Leche*.

CHAPTER IX

NICKNAMES

> I call to mind an Anagram which the Papists made
> of Reverend Calvin,—"*Calvinus Lucianus.*" And now
> they think they have *nicked* the good man to purpose,
> because Lucianus was notoriously known as an Athiest
> and grand Scoffer at the Christian religion.—T. FULLER,
> *The Worthies of England.*

NICKNAMES have been conferred in all ages, and by
people of all nationalities. Even the dullest of races
have used them freely. In the religious controversies of
by-gone ages the opprobrious nickname was a favourite
and effective weapon of offence. The English people
of Plantagenet times like their neighbours in France,
Germany and Italy, were fond of exercising their wits
by inventing these. The evidence of this is to be found
in the Directories of each of these countries, which are
crowded with nickname surnames. The Saxons made
use of them, but they were not so apt in the art as the
Normans, and lacked the rough humour and keenness
of observation that often made the verbal inventions
of their successors so apposite. None escaped the
shafts of the nickname maker, and even Royalty was
not exempt. Some of these verbal titles were complimentary, but more often they were tinctured with
malice. At times they were outrageously offensive.
The most dignified and fastidious could not object to

such names as *le Beauclerk*, *Rufus*, *Fairfax* or *Freman* (Freeman). But the names *Frog*, *Freshfish*, *Bald*, *Hoggesflesh*, *Drynk-Ale*, *Drunkard*, *Drybread*, *Half-naked*, *Losewit*, *Milksop*, *Pennyfather*, *Pinchpenny*, *Two-penny*, *Two-year-old* and *Wrangservice* could scarcely be described as complimentary though none of them are worse than the term *Crookbacked* which was freely applied to one of the Angevin Kings. Yet these and many other surnames equally uncouth are to be met with in old records. Thus in the Calendar of Coroners' Rolls of the City (London) A.D. 1300-1378, we learn that at an Inquest held on the wife of Richard of Barstaple that this woman who was *enceinte* was met in the High Street near the Tower by Agnes *Houdy-doudy*, that a quarrel arose between the women, the said Agnes struck and kicked the other and then fled.

In the same Rolls the names John *Gamon*, John *Drake* and William *Bullock* appear as members of a jury ; while at an inquest held on the death of Thomas *Skylful*, two members of the jury are Alan le *Wolf* and Nicholas *Quaynte*. *Wolf* is an animal nickname ; *Quaynte* the source of which is *cognitus*, and afterwards Old French *coint*, meaning *tasteful* or *tidy* appears in the old Rolls as *Coynte* and *Queynte*. It figures among modern surnames as *Quint*. In this Calendar appear the names Edmund *Trentemars*, William *Halpund*, Robert *Halpenny*, Bartholomew *Deumars*. These are all *money* names that may be compared with others. Thus in the Hundred Rolls the name Fulco *Twelpence* is entered, while the Writs of Parliament contains that of Robert *Peny*. In the fourteenth century a John

Twentimark was Rector of Risingham in Norfolk. Other strange looking names of this class are *Fourpeni*, *Fivepeni*, *Sixpenni*, *Shilling*, *Manypeni*, *Farthing*, *Threeshilling* and *Ducat*.

Pennyfather is now *Pennefather*, and the modern representative of *Manypeni* is *Moneypenny*. *Penney*, *Penny*, *Farthing* and *Shilling* all make a good show in Directories.

This is not by any means a complete list of money surnames. There is for example the name *Turnpenny*, about which Canon Bardsley in his book on *English Surnames* quotes the following : " The wife of Mr. Turnpenny, newsagent, Leeds, was yesterday delivered of two sons and one daughter, all of whom are doing well. (*Manchester Evening News*, July 1, 1873.) "

These money names serve to show from what strange and inexplicable sources surnames have been derived. And not only are these sources strange and inexplicable —they are also so various that classification is impossible. Even when large groups of these are tabulated many thousands still remain to be accounted for. In deciding on a name for friend or neighbour almost any terms came in useful for the purpose ; and if they had only known Euclid's Definitions they would have used these as freely as Daniel O'Connell when he silenced the Dublin fish-wife's storm of abuse by calling her a right angle and a parallelogram.

Many of these nicknames are descriptive of personal appearance as in Thomas *Thynne* of the Hundred Rolls, and Richard *Stout* of the Writs of Parliament. Others

indicate physical peculiarities, e.g. Joscelin le *Strong*,
Amice *Swift*, *Dent-de-fer*, i.e. Iron-toothed, *Gentilcorps*,
or Handsome body.

In the Calendar of the City Coroners' Rolls (Roll E)
we read that John de Otway took refuge in the church
of St. Botulph near Byllyngsgate on July 13, 1326,
" and confessed before the Coroner and Sheriffs that
he was a thief, having taken £10 out of the coffers of
Sir Thomas *Gentilcorps* at Kyngestone . . . He
refused to surrender and abjured the realm."

Degrees of relationship are indicated in the surnames
Kinsman, *Parent*, *le Neve*, nephew. In this group there
are many names. Others again express mental and
moral qualities, as Duran le *Bon*, and Thomas *Doughtye*,
from which our *Bones*, *Bunns* and *Doughtys* spring.

Nicknames are also derived from different parts of
the human frame as in *Head*, *Beard*, *Nose* and *Mouth*.
Some of these are recorded as William *Heved* (Writs of
Parliament), Hugo cum Barba (Hundred Rolls),
Richard Merrymouth (Riley's *Memorials of London*).
The name *Head* is often local as well as a nickname.
It is also an element in many compound nicknames
like *Fairhead* and *Redhead* (William *Fairhead* and John
Redheved, both in the Hundred Rolls).

Colour names are also amazingly numerous. Of
these the commonest are *Black*, *Brown* and *Grey*.
(Ederick le *Blacke*, Wymara *Brown* and John le *Grey*.
All to be seen in the Hundred Rolls.) Needless to say
these are among the most popular of modern surnames.

The peasant of medieval England lived in closer touch with Nature than his modern descendants. The mighty forests in which the King and his nobles hunted were the refuges for outlaws and masterless men. From the woods which were never far from town and village settlements the bondman supplemented his scanty store of food and fuel, and he knew much concerning the beasts and birds that inhabited them. And this familiarity was of service to him and his fellows in finding appropriate nicknames. From Beasts and Birds alone we derive quite an imposing list of surnames, and this is supplemented by many more taken from the names of Flowers, Fruit, Vegetables and Fishes. Some of these are undoubtedly taken from shop signs and heraldic devices, for in the Middle Ages every tradesman and merchant hung out his sign which generally bore some symbolic device. Of this ancient method of advertising the barber's pole, the three golden balls of Lombardy and the Inn signs are the sole survivors. The Inn signs are plentiful and diverse enough to merit the attention of all students of antiquarian lore. Among them we find such names as The Golden Lion, The Goat and Compasses, The Bald Faced Stag, The Dunny Duck, The Hare and Hounds, The Bear, The Eagle, The Bull, The Ram, The Falcon, and The Swann. The majority of craftsmen had signs which were generally appropriate to their own trade, though occasionally they were fanciful. From these many nicknames were derived.

Of wild animals the names *Bear*, *Wolfe* and *Squirrel*

are typical. These figure in the Hundred Rolls as Elina le *Wolfe*, Richard le *Bere* and le *Squirrel*.

As might be expected the farmyard has been freely drawn upon, of which the records furnish many examples as *Steer*, *Calf*, *Hog* and *Mutton*.

Among bird nicknames we find *Star* and its diminutive *Starling*, *Falcon*, *Titmus* and *Jay*. All of these appear in the early records in spelling that seems a little more eccentric than our own, but the names are indubitably the same.

Fish names, to give only a brief list, are represented by *Whiting*, *Salmon*, *Herring* and *Pike*, while among flower names the most popular are *Daisy*, *Bloom*, *Blanchflower* and *Primrose*.

Peculiarities of dress have also furnished their quota as we find in names like *Whittle*, meaning blanket, *Letherhall*, *Curtmantel*, *Tabard*, *Gai-cote* and *Wolleward*. Here again we find indications of the shop sign, especially in the names *Tabard* and *Gai-cote*.

Anyone who studies the Rolls containing particulars of Inquests can hardly fail to be convinced that the rude forefathers of the hamlet were sometimes very rude and lacked the self-control that argues the well-balanced mind. We notice this in the variety of clubs and cudgels they carried—and used—as well as knives. Among these were the *Clubb*, the *Staff* and *Truncheon*, as well as the Pilgrim's Staff the *Burdon*. The names of these old weapons still live in the Directories as surnames.

The precious metals have also furnished the names *Gold* and *Golden* as well as *Silver*.

Implements of all kinds have also made additions to the names list such as *Mallet, Shuttle, File, Rodd, Crook, Horne, Sword, Spear* and *Shotbolte*.

The names of different kinds of sailing vessels like *Ketch* and *Hoy ;* of musical instruments such as *Harp* and *Organ ;* of cereals like *Corn* and *Rye ;* and of articles of food *Cake* and *Drybread* have also made a considerable contribution to the list of " nickname " surnames.

The names of this class already given, if not very dignified, are at least void of offence. But others that must now be mentioned are the reverse of complimentary.

Our English *Drinkwater*, like the German *Trinkwasser*, was no doubt originally a term of derision for one who unlike his neighbours had no strongly developed taste for wine or beer. But those who went to the other extreme received the devastating labels of Geoffrey *Dringhe-dregges* and Robert *le Sot*. *Spare-water* was the name given to a certain Ralph whose ablutions were too perfunctory and sketchy to suit the taste of his friends.

Equally offensive were such names as *Catsnose, Pourfish, Piggesflesh, Hellicate* (Hellcat), *Pine-Coffin* and *Doolittle*. That anyone could be induced to acknowledge the names of Agnes *Cattesnose* and Rayner *Piggesflesh* seems strange enough, but that they should have been regarded as settled surnames by the clerks who solemnly entered them in the Writs of Parliament seems amazing. But it is not surprising that the owners of them took other and pleasanter names, for we find that many names of an offensive type became obsolete centuries ago.

Another and even more curious type of surname is that derived from oaths, mottoes and exclamations. It is not a large class, nor is it one that has survived except in one or two instances, but these strange names stand on record in early documents and bear witness to the hard swearing habits of our ancestors. The Normans were particularly addicted to profanity, and freely interlarded their conversation with meaningless oaths. With the Conqueror it was different. When he swore it was with a fervour that made his hearers realise the intensity of his passion. When he heard that York was lost and that three thousand of his followers were slain, he swore " by the splendour of God " to avenge himself on the rebels.

The French, themselves no mean practitioners of the art, professed themselves shocked at the license in language of their neighbours, and their favourite name for the Englishman was Jean *Goddano*. In the writings of Robert of Braune swearing is alluded to as a conspicuous vice among Englishmen, and in Chaucer most of the characters add emphasis to their speeches by using mouth-filling oaths.

Chaucer himself seems to have had little sympathy with those who condemned the practice as the Host's discussion with the parish priest at the end of the Man of Law's " thrifty " tale shows :

> " Sir parish prest," quod he, " for goddes bones,
> Tel us a tale, as was thy forward yore.
> I see wel that ye lerned men in lore
> Can moche good, by goddes dignitee ! "

The parson was shocked and protested, but the Host in no way abashed, retorted by addressing him as *Jankyn* (little John), and calling him a " loller." Then turning to the company he added darkly :

> " This loller heer wil prechen us som-what."
> " Nay, by my fader soule ! that shal he nat "
> Seyde the Shipman, " heer shal he nat preche."

This habit of interlarding speech with oaths being so common, it is not difficult to understand that men became known by some of the choice and expressive phrases they used. Many years ago there lived in a Cumberland hamlet two worthies who were known respectively as " Shakespeare " and " M'appen I may." The first was so called from his habit of quoting favourite passages from *Hamlet* and *Macbeth*, when in a state of intoxication, the other, who was an excessively cautious individual, received his nickname because whenever he was asked to do anything, his invariable reply was " M'appen I may," which being interpreted means " Happen (or perhaps) I may." There are many such instances of people who have received nicknames through their verbal eccentricities. In the same way those early fathers of our race probably earned their oath names through the constant repetition of certain lurid phrases.

Among these verbal relics of a more profane age we find in the Hundred Rolls such names as *Alicia Godbodi*, William *Godthanke* and Basilia *Godsowle*. From Strype we learn that a Mr. *Gracedieu* was an incumbent of St. James's Church, Duke Street, N. Our modern *Pardows* and *Pardoes* are representatives of the

Pardieus of the Middle Ages ; the name *Damegod*, meaning " Lord God," occurs in the Writs of Parliament and other records.

Surnames from exclamations and heraldic mottoes originate in the same way. This is not a large class, but it is one of great interest to the student. Among the modern names that spring from it are *Godthanke*, *Goodspeed* and *Rumbelow*.

One point emerges from this preliminary outline of the subject—its importance to the student of Early English life. A nation's ballads, as some writers have observed, express its feelings and spirit. In a lesser degree the same can be said of its names. Many of the words from which these names are framed were, as Professor Weekley has pointed out, in common use centuries before they appeared in literary records. Many of them were carefully inscribed in the Hundred Rolls ninety years or so before Chaucer took his quill in hand to write the *Canterbury Tales*, or Langland indited the ploughman's vision. These names were not the artificial conception of learned chroniclers, but the natural and unstudied expression of the thoughts and feelings of the common people. Many of these names are complimentary and express admiration like *Goodson* or *le Bon*. But the majority, as with modern nicknames, seem to be inspired by sly malice, and display the coiner's shrewdness in seizing on some salient weakness or defect in the bearer's character or person. But in all there was an attempt—perhaps unconsciously made—to place names and their owners in a closer and more intimate relation, so that the name given was not a mere label given to distinguish this individual from another, but that it also described and fitted him.

Nearly all the uncomplimentary nicknames as we might naturally expect, have long since disappeared. Those that are flattering still grace the Directories.

CHAPTER X

Names from Pastimes

> Therefore to ride cumlie : to run faire at the tilte
> or ring : to plaie at all weapones : to shote faire in
> bowe, or surelie in gon : to vaut lustely : to runne :
> to leape : to wrestle : to swimme : To daunce cumlie :
> to sing and play of instruments cunnyngly : to hawke :
> to hunt : to playe at tennes and all pastimes generally,
> which by joyned with labor . . . conteining either
> some fitte exercise for warre or some pleasant pastime
> for peace be not onelie cumlie and decent, but also
> verie necessarie.—ROGER ASCHAM, *The Scholemaster*.

THE peasant of the Middle Ages had an unenviable lot.
He was shamelessly robbed by his overlord ; the Reeve,
the Hayward, and the Beadle reduced his scanty
earnings by fines and seizures.   The miller pilfered his
corn.   He was compelled every day to devote hours to
unremunerative toil.

But this state of semi-slavery, though it impaired,
did not destroy his vitality, and he was ever ready to
snatch at any fleeting pleasures that came his way.
Jugglers, wandering minstrels, and Punch and Judy
shows afforded him a childish pleasure ; he was a
regular patron of the Miracle play, but above all else
he was devoted to outdoor sports.

The Baron and Knight found excitement on the
tilting ground, and the commoner, as every reader of

Sir Walter Scott knows, had a passive share in these pleasures. Stow, in his *Annals*, speaks of " very solemn jousting of all the stout earls, barons, and nobles at London in Cheape betwixt the great cross, and the great conduit nigh Soper Lane, which lasted three days, where the Queen Phillipa with many ladies, fell from a stage . . ."

But the people had also their own sports. Archery was as popular then as football is today, and every village youth practised assiduously at the butts or shot at the popinjay so that he might win renown at the trials of skill which took place on feast days.

The English archers had wiped out the stain of Senlac at Tenchebrai. At Cressy and Agincourt they won enduring fame.

It may be that the introduction of firearms caused a lessening of interest in this grand old sport when the first Tudor Kings sat on the Throne. For Skelton in *The Maner of the World* sings :

> So proude and so gaye,
> So riche in arraye,
> And so skant of mon-ey
>   Saw I never :
> So many bowyers
> So many fletchers
> And so few good archers
>   Saw I never.

But we cannot trust Henry VIII's Laureate in this, for he was an incurable satirist and heedless enough to shoot some of his deadliest shafts at the King's powerful minister—Cardinal Wolsey.

From these sports we derive a number of interesting

surnames. The wooden popinjay, already mentioned, at which the archers shot their arrows, was known to Chaucer and his contemporaries as the *papejay*. From this mark we have the uncommon name *Pobgee*.

The accoutrements of the Knights who fought in the tournaments provide many interesting nicknames. The meanings of some of these are so obvious that they require no explanations. Among these are *Vizard*, *Lance*, *Sword*, *Gauntlett* and *Dagger*. The second of these is often a shortened form of Lancelot. From *Shelde*, Shield, we get our modern names *Shield* and *Shields*. Many knights wore a *caplin* or *capeline*, from which the surname *Chaplin* is derived. In the City Rolls we find names of craftsmen indispensable to the man-in-armour, Philip *Sporier* and Symekyn *Sadeler*.

From the other great sport of kings and nobles we have first the names *Hunt* and *Hunter*. Early forms of these names are recorded in the Hundred Rolls as Nicholas le *Hunte* and Henry le *Huntere*, and in the Writs of Parliament as Gilbert le *Hunt* and Thomas le *Hunter*, from which it will be seen that the modern form is almost identical with that of the records. There is also an entry in the Hundred Rolls of the name Walter *Hunteman*, the forerunner of our present *Huntsman*. The French *veneur* has in the surname Directory become *Venner* or *Fenner*, and *Grantvenor*, afterwards modified to *Grosvenor* means the great hunter or Royal Huntsman.

Tod is a north-country word for fox, and is widely known by this name in Scotland. This word forms the first element in the surname *Todhunter*, one of the very few compounds with *hunter* that survive. The name Richard *le Wolfhunt* is entered in the Hundred Rolls, but the name seems to have disappeared.

In the name *le Hunderd*, the present form of which is *Hunnard*, we are reminded of the responsible member of the staff who had charge of the dogs. The *Venterer* or as he is now called *Feuterer* slipped them.

Among several officials who were responsible for keeping the woods in order and protecting the game were the parkmen from whom have come to us the names *Park*, *Parker* and *Parkman* ; the early forms being *Parc*, *atte Parke* (local).

The name *Chaser*, which appears in the Hundred Rolls, is now obsolete, but *Chase* is now frequently met with.

Warren was then as now a common surname. It is local, as the name *de Waren* indicates. But *Warner* and *Warener* are occupative as the names Jacke *le Warner* and William *le Warrener* in the Hundred Rolls show. *Warner* and *Warrener*—the modern forms—are numerous.

Forester, in spite of the competition of the shortened forms, *Forster* and *Foster*, has to a certain extent maintained its ground. But the short forms are naturally much more numerous. In the City Rolls of the fourteenth century the *Forsters* far outnumber the other two. Now *Foster* has taken the premier place.

The *Woodrofe* or *Woderove*, now Woodroff, representing the wood-reeve, were colleagues of the officers already mentioned.

John le *Haukere*, of the Writs of Parliament, was either in charge of, or a dealer in these sporting birds, so that from this pastime we get the names *Hawke*, *Hawker*, *Falcon*, *Falconer*, though Falcon is often personal from *Fulc*, the font name borne by the Dukes of Anjou.

Other names connected with the chase are *Wildbare* and *Wilgress* (for *grice*), *Wildrake* and *Wildgoose*, *Palfreyman*, *Sellar* and *Seller* are at times occupative for saddler, as well as local for cellar. A *Fewster* or *Fuster* made the wooden frames of the saddle, and all the names given above have become surnames.

A few rare and curious names that refer more or less directly to the chase are *Chasehare*, *Cullabere* (Kill bear, Mid. English *cullen*, to kill), *Cullahare*, *Draweswerd* (Drawsword). The last of these is found as Henry *Draweswerd* in the Hundred Rolls, and Maurice *Draugheswerd* in the Writs of Parliament.

The surnames derived from archery have already been given in the previous chapter, but it may be mentioned that although the bow has long since been laid aside as a weapon of war, it has ever since the Middle Ages provided a pleasant pastime for young people. In London that company known as the Finsbury Archers which can boast a respectable antiquity, and the Archers' Company of the Honourable Artillery Company are the proud possessors of a shield presented to them by Queen Catherine of Braganza.

The Company of Royal Archers in Edinburgh, who wear a picturesque green uniform, possesses high social status, and to obtain a place in its ranks is by everyone

11

regarded as a great privilege. When the Sovereign visits Holyrood this Company provides his guard of honour.

At the annual archery contests which are held every year by the Woodmen of Arden the winner of the bugle has to present a purse of shillings to the woman who draws the lucky number in a lottery, and the arrows used on this occasion are marked, in accordance with ancient usage, according to their weight in silver money.

Dancing was a popular amusement of our forefathers. Indeed it was so much indulged in by the peasants in the precincts of local churches that the clergy often complained of the noise and disturbance when services were held. But the pastime has left only a few surnames to commemorate those joyous exercises of long ago. The chief of these are *Dance* and *Dancer*. The second of these was much the more popular and appears in the Hundred Rolls as *Hervens le Danser*. In the Calendar of Proceedings in Chancery the name is spelt *Dawnser*.

We have also *Leaper* and *Hopper*, but the former is probably more associated with jumping than dancing. Of the latter there are both *Hopper* and *Hopperson*. In the Hundred Rolls the name Richard *le Hoppar* is entered and in other old records we find Geoffrey le *Hoppere* and Adam le *Hoppere*. This surname remains to us, practically unchanged.

Saltier does not always mean a trader in salt. Shakespeare uses the term as a corruption of Satyr, with some reference, as Smythe Palmer says in *Folk Etymology* to the Latin *saltare*, to dance, French *salace*, to leap. So that *Salterer* may at times mean dancer as well as William *le Tumbere* of the Writs of Parliament whose name is French from *tombeur*. The name *Burder* presents a problem. The verb *bourd* to jest, is used by Ford, and frequently occurs in Caxton's *Reynard the Fox*. In the *Proloug of the XII Buk of Encados*, by Garvin Douglas, we read :

> " Smyland " says one, " I couth in previte
> Schaw the a *bourd*." " Ha quhat be that ? " quod he ;
> " Quhat thyng ? that most be secrete," said the tother.

Bourd is from Old French, a jest, and the surname *Burder* may, in some instances at least, be derived from the wag or jester. We have also the surname *Jester*, but the duty of the person who originally filled the position implied by this name, was that of a story-teller.

CHAPTER XI

Nicknames of Dispositions

Many of the nicknames which indicate mental and moral qualities are adjectival, and a considerable proportion highly complimentary. Much as we admire those sturdy ancestors of ours for their patient endurance of conditions which their descendants would regard as appalling, we never suspected them of being " faultily faultless," or for the possession of qualities that would entitle them to be enrolled in the calendar of saints. Yet when we read their names, names obviously conferred by friends and neighbours, for no one would deliberately adopt such names themselves— we wonder that men of such pure and blameless life endured existence among people so full of original sin. To take an example or two at random we find families rejoicing in such names as *Perfect*, *Faithful* and *Good*. When Hugh Godde (Good) of the Hundred Rolls, and Roger Godde of the Writs of Parliament, disclosed their names to the enquiring officials they must have done so with a smile of self-conscious worth that broke down the icy reserve of those dignified officials. The modern *Goods* have reason to be proud of the original who established the surname. *Faultless* must have been an admirable man, but a little too awe-inspiring for easy companionship, though he might conceivably be a much better fellow than *Best*, for this term is relative and might not represent a very high standard. There are many *Bests* in the records—Richard *le Best* of the Hundred Rolls, Henry *le Beste* of Riley's *Memorials*, and others. Many people today bear the honourable name they founded.

But these paragons were not lonely in their rarified atmosphere of virtue for they had the company of *Sage* and *Wise*, *Mercy* and *Blythe*, *Sweet* and *Meek*, though some of these, notably *Wise*, *Mercy* and *Meek* are Pageant names. *Truman* and *Goodhart* also serve as reminders of the Miracle plays.

Whatever the origin of these names there is little doubt that some of them were ironically applied to individuals who posed before their neighbours as people of lofty character and superior intelligence.

Snel, from Anglo-Saxon, means courageous as well as swift. *Sharp* and *Smart* are equally complimentary.

Frek and *Frike*, found respectively in the Writs of Parliament and Hundred Rolls, are names of honour, for they denote, not eccentricity, as might be supposed from one of its present representatives—*Freak*, but valour and manliness. It is from A. Saxon *frec*, bold, daring, whence *freca*, a bold one, Old English *freke*, a man, a knight. Minot uses the adjective in his Political songs :

> Oure King and his men helde the felde
> Stalworthy, with spere and schelde,
> And thoght to win his right,
> With lordes and with knightes kene
> And other doghty men bydene
> That war ful *frek* to fight.

In addition to *Freak* there still survive a *Frick* and *Freke*. The Old French adjective *prena*, meaning valiant, has given us a number of surnames including *Prew*, *Prue*, *Prow* and *Prowse*.

The poet Keats owed his name to Osbert *le Ket*, meaning the bold.

The Teutonic *Earp*, swarthy, from a compound of which—*Earpwine*—we get the name of the famous artist, Sir William Orpen, was also the origin of the famous medieval name *Orpede*, now very rare as *Orped*.

The surname *Parfitt* reminds us of the former pronunciation and form of the word which has been discarded in favour of that orthographical abomination *perfect*.

John Doughtye is easy to identify, as are also John *de la Bold* and Thomas *Galaunt* of the Hundred Rolls, and John *Vygerous* of Riley's *Memorials*. *Doughty* and *Bold* are almost unchanged, while Vygerous has become *Vigars*.

Parfey, which was an oath name, has changed in form, and as *Purefoy* advertises its bearer's orthodoxy.

We find English and French equivalents in *Goodheart*, *Goodhart*, and *Bonquer* for *Bon-cœur*, which in the modern name has been shortened to *Bunker*.

The French *Bon* which yielded the surnames *Bone*, *Bune* and *Boon* is also the origin of *Bunn*, the name of the so-called poet who in Victorian days penned the lyrics of popular Italian operas, and that of the Marian bishop, *Bonner*.

The names *Hendy* and *Hendiman* are interesting, for they keep alive among our surnames an old word that has become obsolete. Its original meaning is handy, but as one who acted *hendliche*, i.e. handily, also did it politely the word *hende* gained the secondary meaning of *urbane* or *courteous*. It is used in this sense by Chaucer in the *Canterbury Tales* and in *Peres the Ploughman's Creed* the adverb *hendliche* is used with the same meaning.

" I hayesede that herdeman and hendliche y saide."

In the City Letter Book, No. 1, it is recorded that in 1404 John *Hende* was elected Mayor for the year ensuing. The name is also found in other records, while William Hendeman's name is entered in the Hundred Rolls.

Names like *Gentilman, Curteis* or *Curtis* were inspired either by a spirit of mockery or were coined by people who hoped to profit by flattery. It is also of course probable that some at least of these verbal bouquets were given in good faith, but as in those days, like our own, there were flatterers and mockers as well as those who appreciated solid worth, it is more than likely that these complimentary names came from all three sources.

Words, as those who have more than a nodding acquaintance with etymology know, have an awkward trick of changing their meanings, and names that sounded gracious and pleasing to their original owners, are looked upon as dubious by their successors. The original meaning of Sad was serious, and Robert *Sad* whose name appears in the Rolls of Parliament had no reason to believe that his surname suggested a gloomy or pessimistic nature. The Hundred Rolls includes among its many names Jordan *le Simple*, and so does the Writs of Parliament. The meaning of this adjective, like the German *schlecht*, has profoundly changed. *Simple* originally meant without guile, and such a person in religious communities was regarded as a pattern and example for others. But as this simplicity exposed its owner to the cunning and artifice of the unscrupulous, he gradually came to be regarded as one deficient in the qualities that make for success in life, or to put the point tersely, as a *simpleton*. The German *schlecht* also at first meant simple but its meaning changed in a different way. There the simple man though at first regarded as without guile and in consequence mercilessly imposed on, was at last compelled to meet deceit with the guile of Bret Hart's Heathen Chinee, so that *schlecht* acquired a new significance and meant *bad* or *evil*. From this, then, it is plain that *simple* was a name that none of its owners cared to own.

The old adjective *sely*, meaning good, simple, innocent, has firmly embedded itself in our surname Roll. But here again the meaning of the word has greatly changed. It is from Anglo-Saxon *Sælig*, happy, German *selig*, but its meaning in modern English is *silly*, and the story of its change of meaning is almost identical with that of the word *simple*. The *sely* man, innocent and unwary, was no match for those who cheated and tricked him at every turn, and the world cynically shook its wise old head over him and changed the adjective that described him from *sely* to *silly*.

Of names derived from *sely* we find William *Sely* in the Hundred Rolls, and Benedict *Sely* and George

Selyman in the *Cal. Rotul. Chartarum*, and to these and others who bore these names in the early centuries we owe the names *Seeley*, *Sealey*, *Selyman*, *Silly* and *Sillyman*.

Before turning to other words it may be remarked that an overwhelming mass of evidence as to the meaning attached to the word *sely* could be adduced. Chaucer himself uses it more than once, and always in this sense. In the *Clerke's Tale*, Group E, we learn that the " markis "

> sente his message
> For thilke *sely* poure Griselde ;
> And she with humble herte and glad visage,
> Nat with no swollen thought in her corage,
> Cam at his heste.

Sly and *Cunning* are also words that have fallen from their former high estate. In Early English *cunning* was another word for knowledge, and *sly* meant skilful, and it is due to the fact that many of those who possessed the skill and knowledge that marked them out from their fellows took unfair advantage of them that the words acquired sinister meanings.

The surnames *Sly* and *Sleigh*, *Slee*, *Slemman* and *Slyman* and possibly *Slay* are a legacy from people like Richard *Sle* (Hundred Rolls), Simon le Slegh (Writs of Parliament), John *le Slège* (Hundred Rolls), Davy *Sleman* (Cal. of Proceedings in Chancery—Elizabeth), John *Slye* (Rolls of Parliament). These names in their turn are from the M. English adjective *slegh*, meaning sly, skilful.

high as surnames, and maintain their standing in the Directories.

When surnames first became hereditary the term *paramour* suggested nothing discreditable and signified no more than the man in love, so that though Roger *Paramour* of the Writs of Parliament might be a little sensitive in being made through this nickname the butt of his neighbours' jests, he had little reason to be ashamed of the name they had given him. Since that time the term has taken an unpleasant meaning which would have caused discomfort to its modern bearers if the original form of the word had not been partly disguised by the addition of an *r* to the first syllable, thus making the name *Parramore*.

Lemman is from Anglo-Saxon *leof-man*, literally a dear person, *man* being of either gender, as in *wifman*, a woman. This word also lost its original meaning and *lemman* or *leman* became a term of contempt for a woman of loose character. Chaucer uses the word in its original sense when in the *Monk's Tale* he says of Samson :

> Unto his lemman Dalida he tolde
> That in his heres (hair) all his strengthe lay,
> And falsly to his foomen she him solde.

The word is now obsolete as a counter in conversation but it survives in the surnames *Leman*, *Lemon* and *Lemman*, whose owners have no more reason to be ashamed of them than Eldred *Leman* of the Hundred Rolls had, when he first received the nickname.

We have also the French equivalent of Well-beloved, mentioned in a previous paragraph, in *Bienayme* and

Bonamy, both of which are in the Hundred Rolls. *Bienayme* has become obsolete, but *Bonamy* is yet a well known surname.

OBJECTIONABLE CHARACTER NICKNAMES

In the French, German and Italian Directories there are multitudes of nickname surnames and many of these are definitely uncomplimentary. So it is with our English names.

Some of these names are incredibly offensive. Robert *le Sot* and Geoffrey *Dringkedregges* have been mentioned in a previous chapter, but there are others equally libellous. In the Hundred Rolls one unfortunate is branded as Henry *le Lyare*, while in another entry of the same document we find Stephen *le Gabber* which conveys the same meaning, for the Promptorium Parvulorum has the definition " Lyare or *gabbare*— *mendax, mendosus*. But these downright terms do not quite express the meaning of the name. Wicklyffe speaks of gabbing as lying, but he was a strict moralist and regarded light conversation as empty babble. In the English translation of *The Romance of King Alexander* made about 1300 A.D. the word *gabbe* is used in the sense of joking. It comes from Anglo-Saxon *gabban*, to scoff, delude, while the Mid. English *gabben* is from Old French *gaber*, to mock. From this we may infer that *Gabber* meant what in certain refined circles is known as a " leg-puller."

Among uncomplimentary nicknames we also find the name *Ribote* or *Ribaud*. A ribaud was a gentleman whom no one would care to know—an idle profligate. But the word is very interesting to etymologists, for it has travelled far and in its wanderings has little altered in form and meaning. It is from Old French *riboult*, Mid. H. German *ribalt*. Skeat suggests that ribalt in its turn is from M.H.G. *ribe* Old H. German *kripe*, a prostitute, hence, perhaps English *rip*.

Again among these early names appears *Lusk*, evidently first conferred on some lazy, worthless fellow by those who knew his character, for *luske* was a Mid English term for lazy. The word was in use for centuries and employed by the Elizabethan dramatists, but has long been obsolete like the *lorells* with which it was classed. But the name has been borne by so many people of character and reputation that it is deservedly held in honour.

The name *Levegood* of the City Letter Books suggests that the original owner of the name was one who had abandoned a life of virtue, while *Levelyf* may have belonged to one who had abjured the world and its vanities.

Turnpenny and *Torngold* or *Torgold* evidently refer to people who had been successful in gathering gear, and stand out in contrast to *Whirlpenny* which indicates the spendthrift, Gilbert le *Covetiose*, appears in the Writs of Parliament, though none now bear the name.

NICKNAMES OF RELATIONSHIP

Surnames formed from terms of relationship illustrate one of the simplest methods of forming surnames. It is similar to that in which patronymics were adopted.

In the Introductory chapter a document was quoted, from which it appeared that all the members of one family had adopted different surnames. But even when these had been taken, it is highly probable that " neighbours or acquaintances when speaking of them would refer to the uncle, the brother or the cousin of John rather than use the new fangled surname. In many cases, of course, the surname would survive, but in others the term of relationship would become the surname. Bardsley quotes one record that admirably illustrates this : " *John Darcy le fiz*, John *Darcy le frere*, John *Darcy le unkle*, John *Darcy le cosyn*, John *Darcy le nevue* and John *Darcy, junior*."

In any case many of these names were adopted. Some have become obsolete, but many survive. Thus in the Hundred Rolls we find both John *le Uncle* and Richard *le Cusyn*. Many of these names of kinship have an added *s* as in *Cousins, Cozens, Brothers, Sones,* and *Mothers*.

From the Mid. English *eme*, uncle (from Anglo-Saxon *eam*) we get the names *Eame, Ames, Eme* and *Neame*. As well as *Brothers* there is the French equivalent *Frere*. The Mid. English word for nephew, *neve*, has contributed the surname *Neave* and *Neaves*. It is interesting to note that this Old English term was passing out of use at the close of the fourteenth century, for we find Chaucer employing the term *nevew*, from the Old French accusative *neveu*. From the nominative of this word *niés* the rare surname *Neese* comes.

The word *child* was in the Middle Ages a common term of address to a young man. In Chaucer's *Sir*

Thopas the giant says to the knight who has ventured into his domain

Child, by Termagaunt
But if thou prike out of myn haunt,
Anon I sel thy stede
With Mace.

The poet also speaks of the prophet Daniel as " the wysest child of everychoon."

So *Child* figures among surnames, as well as its Anglo-French equivalent *Faunt*, an aphetic form of *enfaunt*. The surnames *Fant* and *Vant* are also from *Faunt*. *Faunt* is more familiar to moderns in the compound *Fauntleroy*, meaning *Kingson*, which as a surname has got mixed up with the local name *Kingston*.

The Hundred Rolls records Arnold le *Fader*, and the Writs of Parliament John *Faderless*, while the former document also has the name *Parent*, a French word of Latin origin. Bardsley quotes from a Cambridge register of 1544 the remarkable name John *Orphanstrange*. This we need hardly add is one that has not survived.

Widdows and *Widdowson*, which appeared in the Hundred Rolls as Simon *fil. Vidue* and William *fil. Wydo* are yet prosperous surnames.

Barnfather and *Bairnsfather* are well-known surnames in Scotland and the north of England. For Bairn or *Barn* the dialect name for a child is Old English *bearn* (Anglian *barn*). From this term comes the well-known surname *Barnes*, which in the Hundred Rolls appears as William *le Barne*. But *Barnes* is also local and indicates residence at or near a barn, for in the document just quoted from we find the name Warin *de la Barne*.

From Walter *Bonenfant* of the Hundred Rolls comes the surname *Bonifant* which has its English parallel in the name *Goodchild*.

Gayfer and *Belcher* (from Old French *bel-sire*) are for grandfather as *Beldam* is for grandmother. The surname *Odam* is letter for letter the Mid. English term for son-in-law.

Male has the same meaning as *Maskelyne* which is from French *masculin*=Latin *masculinus* extended from *masculus*, male.

In *Wills and Inventories* (Lancashire) appears the name Thomas *Twoyearold*. The name is still to be found in north country Directories.

Sire for father has also furnished the surnames *Sirr* and *Syre*. The Hundred Rolls has Alexander *le Sire* and Manimenta. Gildh. Lond., William *le Syre*. The name also appears as the second element of *Goodsir*, *Sweetsur* and *Dunsire*.

NICKNAMES FROM PHYSICAL ATTRIBUTES

Nicknames from physical features are both complimentary and otherwise, but they are all, like most nicknames, remarkable for frankness. Some were politely called *Bigg*, *Large*, *Thick*, *Round*, *Fatt* and *Stout*. Others by some master of picturesque phrase were dubbed *Broadbelt*, *Pudding* and *Mucklebone*, the last of which appears in the Hundred Rolls. We also find the descriptive names *Light*, *Lean*, *Megre*, *Little*, *Thin* and *Slight*.

12

In these lists we find both English and their French equivalents. Thus *Large*, *Bigg*, *Little* or *Lowe* are confronted with *Gros*, *Grand* or *Grant*, *Petty* or *Pettitt*, *Bas* or *Bass*. A few of these are now obsolete, but the majority have seen service, and may be found in many Directories.

Some of these adjectival surnames are also found in the comparative and even superlative degree, as in *Littler* and *Least*, *Shorter* and *Stronger*, *Old* and *Elder*.

It is only, however, when we descend from the general to the particular and consider the long list of nicknames formed from the separate joints, members and muscles of the human frame that we marvel at the ingenuity and knowledge of our forefathers. For here we have an anatomical schedule of the different parts of the body that is not more remarkable for its flippancy and impertinences than for its fulness. The *Foot*, the *Head*, the *Limb*, the *Tooth* and many more find a place in the roll of surnames. But it is necessary to look at these, as all other names, critically, and not to accept them unthinkingly at their face value.

The need for caution becomes evident when we consider *Heved* as *Head*. For *Head* is often local as in Thomas *del Heved* of the Hundred Rolls, for *of the Head* probably refers to the fact that Thomas lived at the head of a valley or hamlet.

There are many compounds of *head*, among which are Richard Wetherherd, *Weatherhead* (Hundred Rolls), Antony *Wiselheade* for *Weaselhead* (Calendar of Pleadings, Elizabeth), Thomas *Gretehed*, for Greathead

(Rolls of Parliament), William *Fairheved, Fairhead*
(Hundred Rolls). *Sheepshead*, which may be compared
with *Weatherhead* mentioned above, was the name of
the Abbot of Leicester in 1474.

But this does not exhaust the compounds of *head ;*
for we find also *Coxhead* or *Cockshead, Downyhead,
Shavenhead, Goldenhead, Rufhead* and even *Greenhead*.
Those who are familiar with John Bunyan's history
know that it was at the house of Josias *Roughead* in
Bedford that Bunyan first received his licence to
preach in 1672.

Mouth from M. English *mouth*, Anglo-Saxon *mūs*,
figures among our surnames as well as the French *bouche*
as in the surnames *Bouch* and *Buche*. *Merymouth* is a
name often found in the old records.

Nose may sometimes be a nickname, but in Roger
atte Ness of the Hundred Rolls *ness* is local and means
a headland.

Hand and *Hands* are nicknames as well as pet forms.
Matilda *Finger* of the Rolls of Parliament has left no
modern successors.

Arm is found in several compounds as well as the
simplex *Armes*, and we find the well-known *Armstrong*
as in William *le Armstrang* (*Calen. Rotul. Originalium*)
and *Strongetharm*. The French *bras* also survives in
compounds like *Firebrace*, an early form of which appears
in the Writs of Parliament as *Ferbras*.

Main or *Mayne*, the French equivalent for hand,
is generally local, but sometimes it carries its face
meaning as a nickname. In compounds it gives the
surnames *Blanchmaine* and *Quatermains* (Writs of

Parliament). *Leg* is both personal and local. Sometimes it is the shortened form of *Ledger* ; at others it stands for Leigh, one of the several forms of *Lea*, a meadow, but it does not seem to have been used as a nickname. On the other hand *shank* and *shanks* were freely employed by the nicknamer, and the French *jambe* proved equally popular. The compounds of these terms are pointed and often unflattering. *Crookshanks* and its Scottish variant *Cruickshanks* are widely distributed surnames. The name *Sheepshanks* also designates a considerable number of people, though but few now acknowledge the name borne by Gilbert *Greyschanke* of the Hundred Rolls. *Longshanks*, once historic as a nickname, has left no successors among modern surnames.

The best known compounds of *jambe* are *Bellejambe* and *Foljambe*.

Foot has several descriptive compounds. The Hundred Rolls has Peter *Yrensfot* (*Ironfoot*) which is matched by Bernard *Pedefer* of the *Cal. Rotul. Originalium*. From this we get the names *Pettifer* and *Petifer*. We have also *Lightfoot, Harefoot, Crowfoot, Broadfoot, Roefoot, Puddifoot, Grayfoot* and *Proudfoot*.

Nicknames from Costume

From Surnames we have many reminders of the dress worn in medieval times and the materials from which it was fashioned.

To take head-gear first we find in *Plac. de Quo Warranto* the name John *atte Hatt*, and in the Hundred Rolls Thomas *del Hat*. Neither of these seem to be

genuine nicknames.   The first is apparently local, the
second is probably from a shop sign.   In City Letter
Book H, *John Cappe* is mentioned as one of the Masters
of the Mistery of Founders.   In the same record appears
the name *Chapel* which in some examples represents
Old French *chapel*, the equivalent of *chapeau*.

Mantel, the name of a garment which has survived
many centuries of fashion's changes, is strongly
represented in old records.

Eccentricity in dress then, as now, exposed the
wearers to the jibes of the irreverent, for we find several
nicknames beginning with *Curt*, like *Curtepy*, the jacket
Chaucer mentioned and made famous, *Curtmantel* and
Curthose.   But *hose* also forms part of a few compounds
as in *Ledderhose* for *Leatherhose*, *Widehose*, *Shorthose*
and *Goldhose*.

Curthose occasionally survives in its original form,
but generally it has been shortened into *Curtis*.   As this
name also originates in *Curteis*, the polite or courteous,
as we have already pointed out, it is impossible to
decide how any given example of the name arises, but
we can at least understand the cause of its popularity.

Just as *coate* has got hopelessly confused with *cote*,
a cottage, so *hose* has been mixed up with *house* ; and
as it seems impossible to know whether anyone named
Coates owes his name to a dwelling, or an article of
attire the same difficulty arises when the names *Hose*
or *House* are considered.   Thus *Widehose* and *Shorthose*
in some instances may stand for *Widehouse* and
Shorthouse.

Tabard and *Taber* are names that remind us of the

garment that was worn not only by the herald, but in much more modest fashion by the peasantry as well.

In the Hundred Rolls there appears the interesting surname *Woleward*, which in other old documents is also spelt *Wolleward* and *Wollward*. This term serves as a reminder of one of the penances imposed by the Church, when one who had confessed his transgressions had " to go woolward," i.e. in wool only—without linen. Palsgrave's definition runs, " Wolworde, without any lynnen nexte ones body, *sans chemyse*." In his *Annals*, H7 (Nares) Stow speaks of one who went woolward and barefooted to many churches. In *Peres The Ploughman's Crede*, we find in line 788 :

> And werchen and wolward gon as we wrecches usen.

In *The Glossary of Tudor and Stuart Words*, collected by Professor Skeat, edited by A. L. Mayhew, it is suggested that the form *wolleward* " is due to popular etymology, and that the word properly represents an O.E. *wullwered*, clothed in wool. . . . The corruption would be natural when the sense of *wered* was lost, as *ward* was a common suffix."

Woolward is still a familiar surname.

Woollett has nothing to do with wool or dress. It is from the Saxon personal name Wulfgeat (wolf-gate).

When not a local name *Burrel* which appears in *Placita de Quo Warranto* as Roger *Burrell* comes to us from the name of the coarse cloth that many of the poor people wore in medieval times. The Mid. English name for this was *borel* from Old French *burel*. The word acquired the secondary meanings of unlearned, rude and rustic, and *borel men* was used as a rather contemptuous term for laymen.

Blanket is a surname often found in early documents as well as its variant *Blanchet*.

Like *burel*, *blanket* was the name of a coarse, woollen cloth, but in contrast to other materials of similar quality it was pale and colourless, hence the name. *Blanket*, meaning of a white colour, is from M. English *blanket*, from Anglo-French *blanket* (Fr. *blanchet*), a diminutive from *blanc*, white.

Bardsley speaks of *Plunket* as a variant of blankets and regards them as " relics of the time when the colourless woollen mixture, called by these names, was in every-day demand." He adds, in a note, that *plunket* was in early use as a perversion of *blanket*, and states that a statute of Richard III relating to this stuff was called *plonket*. But Bardsley is mistaken in thinking that *blanket* and *plunket* are one and the same material, and he is equally wrong in assuming that the surname *Plunkett* is from *blanket*. Blanket as he states was a colourless woollen mixture, but Plunket was a woollen cloth usually of a grey or light blue colour, just as *porre* is said by Riley to denote a leek-green cloth. In the City Calendar of Pleas and Memoranda Rolls, 1364-1381, there is a detailed account of an action brought by one John Sely against Robert Beauchamp, in which the defendant submitted a list of goods he had handed over to the plaintiff. Among these were—1 Blanket 6s. 8d., 1 Blanket 3s. 4d., and one cloth of *plunket* 66s. 6d. From this evidence it is apparent that blanket and plunket were different materials.

Whittle, a surname common in the north of England, is in meaning closely allied to blanket, and is from Mid. English *Whitel*, a blanket ; A.S. *hwitel*. It is so named for its white colour, as A.S. *hwīt*, means white.

COLOUR AND COMPLEXION NICKNAMES

As colour or complexion offers one of the easiest and readiest methods of identifying the individual, names of this class, though limited in range, account for a considerable proportion of the surnames that crowd the pages of Directories. The two commonest of all nicknames are *White* and *Brown*, and this fact is not without significance, though as explained in a former chapter the names of those who bore the complimentary name *wiht* (the M.E. term for valiant) are now indistinguishable from those that represent the colour.

Among the names in this class are those of *Sor* and *Sorrell*. We find John *le Sor* in the Rolls of Parliament, and Richard *Sorel* in the Writs of Parliament. These names are from the Anglo-French *sor*, reddish brown, and the term was applied to man, beast and bird. Thus a soar-falcon was a hawk of the first year that had not moulted, and still retained its red plumage, while a *sorel* was a reddish-brown horse. The surname *Sor* has disappeared but *Sorel* still lives and prospers.

Dunn is sometimes personal from the Anglo-Saxon *Dunna*. It is also occasionally local, as in Gilbert *atte Dune*, of the Hundred Rolls, but Henry *le Dun* and William *le Dunne* which appear in the same record seem to be the colour nicknames. The term *dun* was in more general use during the surname period than it

is now.   " Dun's in the mire " (the horse is in the mire)
was the name of a popular country game, and the name
of this game passed into popular phraseology.   Chaucer,
Fletcher and Shakespeare all mention it, and Hudibras,
III, 3, 110, Butler, has the line :

> Your trusty squire, who has dragg'd your dunship out o'
> th' mire.

Dun's the mouse was a common jocular phrase in
Tudor days.   From this it is easy to understand how
a man with brown hair or beard acquired the name
Dunn.

Rouse.   A few of the original bearers of this name
may have adopted it from Rollo, the famous Viking
who descended on the French coast and conquered
Normandy ;   or it is the nominative form of *Rou*.   But
the majority must be content with the more prosaic
explanation, that their surname comes from the French
roux, the *red*.   The surname *Rush* is also from this
source.

In the Calendar of City Letter Books, H, there are
frequent references to Richard *Morell*, another colour
name, meaning dark-hued.

From the Saxon *Read* for red we get the surnames
Redd, *Reed*, *Reid* and *Read*.   But these *Reeds* and their
variations are also in some instances from the Mid.
English *ræd*, meaning advice or counsel.

Rudd is also an Anglo-Saxon name from the adjective
Rudda, ruddy.

In the City Letter Books just quoted from appear
the names William *Blount*, Walter *Blund*, Ralph le
Blunt, all of which are from the French *blond*, and

correspond exactly to the English *Fairfax* which means fair haired.   *Blund* is now almost, if not quite, extinct, but its diminutive *Blundell* is a well-known surname. The famous minstrel of legend, *Blondel*, who entertained captive monarchs with sweet melody, might also have boasted that his name was derived from the same source.

A nickname frequently given to the hoary headed was *Hore*.   There are several examples of it in early records.   In 1383 the name of one of the King's Serjeants-at-Arms was Thomas *Hore*.

Bayard and *Bay* were also popular, as were *Grey* and *Black*.   But *Black* and *Blake* though they generally indicate the colour, are also sometimes from Mid. English *blac*, meaning wan of colour, or pale.   Here, then, is an instance where those ignorant and obstinate people who persist in arguing that black is white, may be right for once.

There are a number of descriptive compounds which so clearly define their meaning that they need little or no explanation.   Of these are the surnames *Redhead*, *Whitelock*, *Silverlock*, *Fairhair*, *Blackbeard* and *Greybeard*, all of which still exist though one or two of them, notably *Blackbeard* and *Greybeard*, are anything but common.   In Barrett's *History of Bristol* it is recorded that William Whiteheare was Dean of Bristol in 1551.

NICKNAMES FROM BEASTS, BIRDS AND FISHES

Surnames of this class come to us from two sources. Some were given through shop signs or heraldic devices. Others were conferred because the physical attributes

or supposed characteristics of the animals corre-
sponded in some degree with those of the people on
whom the names were conferred. Those described
from shop signs when the preposition *de la* or *atte*
appear before the surname are easily distinguishable
from the others, as in Gilbert *de la Higle* and Hugh
de Lowe of the Hundred Rolls.

The peasant had many opportunities of increasing
his scanty stores. Medieval England was a land of
dense forests and woods, which had only been partially
cleared by the patient husbandry of Saxon and Danish
settlers. These forests, the refugees of the outlaw and
the masterless man, were also the haunts of the wolf,
the wild boar and many other animals. They provided
unlimited opportunities for those who loved the chase,
and the peasant poached where his master hunted.
John Plowman and his neighbours were experienced
trappers and hunters, but they had strange ideas of the
habits and traits of the beasts they pursued. These
ideas were derived not from observation but tradition.
Curious myths and amazing legends concerning beast
and bird had passed down from generation to generation
and it was from the knowledge of fur and feather this
mass of folk-lore imparted, that the Englishman drew
when he framed nicknames for his acquaintances.

The Beast epics of Reynard, the Fox, in which the
mental and moral qualities of many different animals
were dramatically illustrated, were among the most
popular themes of the minstrels, who roamed the
countryside. These stories were for the unlettered, but
people of all degrees delighted in them, for even the

simplest discovered in them a satiric comment on the abuses of the Church and learnt that cunning and deceit are of greater use in securing worldly advancement than brute force or strength.

The clergy had also in the nature stories of Physiologus a book in which weird and wonderful accounts were given of the beasts of the field. As Mr. James Carlill says in his *Introduction to Physiologus* (" The Epic of the Beast," consisting of English Translations of The History of Reynard the Fox and Physiologus, Broadway Translations, Routledge), this book " formed a great part of the library of Christian Europe for nearly a thousand years. They (the sermons) were read or recited from the Bosphorus to Iceland ; they were quoted by popes and repeated by friars ; they were taught in the universities and schools, were copied in the cloisters, were recited by the fire sides, and were rendered visible to the faithful by carvings in choir or chancel."

This interest in beast and bird is reflected in the long list of surnames derived from this source.

Of the beasts those of the farmyard and the chase were the more familiar and more freely drawn on than any other. Thus we find surnames like Richard *le Bor* in the Hundred Rolls of which the modern equivalent is *Boar ;* Philip *le Hog* (Hundred Rolls), which is now *Hogg ;* Walter *Pigge* from the same record ; William *le Gryse* now found as *Grice* and *Grise.* Like *Grisdale* and *Griswood* already referred to *Gryse* is from Mid. English *gris*, a pig. But *Grice* is also from le *gris*, the grey.

Sugg is from Anglo-Saxon *suga*, sow, and *Purcell* from the Latin *pourceau*. In City Letter Book H, it is stated that in 1378 the plate, jewels, etc., of Richard II were pledged with the City by John Bacoun on the King's behalf.

The entry Alice *le Bule* in the Hundred Rolls looks odd, with the definite article before the surname, but this name was destined to become known to people of all nations as expressing the general characteristics of Englishmen. Equally contradictory are Thomas *le Cu* and its French equivalent Peter *le Vache*.

A sheep in the surname or bi-lingual period was still known to the Anglo-French as *mouton* and the calf as *vean*, and to these terms we owe the well-known surnames *Mutton* and *Veal*. Our *Lambs*, whose early namesakes may be found in the Hundred Rolls, also belong to the same class.

Other farmyard names are *Stot*, *Steer* and *Kidd*. A *stot* represented either a stallion or a bullock and comes from M. English *stot*. *Steer* is from Anglo-Saxon *steor*, a young ox. Among compounds are the names *Wildbore* and *Whitelamb*.

Of names taken from household pets *Catt* and *Katt* are both represented, though the latter is now rare. In the old records they appear indifferently as *Cat*, *Kat* and the French *Chat*. Turning to dogs, we find in the Hundred Rolls the names Thomas *le Chene* and Eborard *le Ken*. The modern surnames are *Ken* and *Kenn*. Associated with these is the nickname *Doggett*, contracted from *Doggisheved*, dog's head. From the cur, M. English *kur-dogge*, the surname *Kerr* is derived.

The surnames *Ratt* and *Ratton* are curious survivals of old nicknames. In the Hundred Rolls the names Nicholas *le Rat* and Ralph *Ratun* both appear. The Mid. English *raton* = French *raton*, diminutive of *rat*.

John le Mous is entered in the Writs of Parliament. Other old forms are *Mowse* and *Mus*.

In the City of London Letter Book H, we find mention of the names of Walter *Buk* or *Bukke*, and his daughter Johanna, the wife of Robert *Faun*. Also those of Stephen *Roo* (*Roe*), John *Raye* (*Ray*) and William *Hare*. The Writs of Parliament also yield Richard le *Hert* (*Hart*), and the Calendar of Pleadings (Elizabeth) Dorothie *Stagg*.

The mention of the polecat reminds us that Chancellors of the Exchequer are not the only despoilers of henroosts, and that this unpleasant animal was anything but popular with owners of poultry. This animal has bequeathed his old name to our surname list in the forms *Fitch* and *Fitchett*. The name Fitchet, Fitchew, a polecat. *Fitchew* is from Picard, *ficheux*, M.F. *fissau* ; the older form *fissel* = Mid. Dutch *fisse*, a polecat. The names *Fitche* and *Fichet* are in the Hundred Rolls and the Writs of Parliament.

The name *le Fox* appears in several ancient records, and is a surname found in many parts of the country. *Todd*, in early documents found as *le Tod* (the fox) is a common name in the northern counties as well as in Scotland.

The modern *Brock* has the same surname, slightly altered, as the *le Brok* and *le Broc* of the thirteenth century records, and he bears the name of the badger.

For the Anglo-Saxon name of the badger was *broc* and it was so called because of its white streaked face.

The beaver has also given the surname *Beaver*, the early forms of which are *le Bever* and *le Bevere*.

From the marten, a kind of weasel, we have the surname *Marten*. The Mid. English name for the otter was *oter* and in this form the name appears in the Hundred Rolls. The modern spelling of the surname is *Otter*.

Some of the wits of the surname period went further afield for their nicknames and bestowed the names of beasts they had never seen on their neighbours, about which they had only the haziest notions. Among these they chose the lion, the tiger, the bear, the leopard and the camel. With the bear they were familiar, as many of these animals had been brought to England from France and were often to be seen at fairs and festivals, where bear-baiting was a popular amusement. Among early surnames *le Bere* (*Bear*), *Barebat* (*Bearbait*), *Barebast* and *Barbast* may all be found in the Hundred Rolls. Of these none but *Bear* have survived. The majority of the *Lions*, *Leopards* and *Tigers* of the records are probably from shop-signs or heraldic devices, but it matters very little from what source the nicknamer derived his inspiration. It is sufficient to know that these names were bestowed and that John *Lepard* of the Rolls of Parliament has left a surname which his namesakes of later centuries have changed to *Leppard*.

But *Oliphant* for elephant is a nickname. It was conferred on the giant who confronted Sir Thopas in

Chaucer's tale *Of Mirthe and of Solas*. In James I's
The Kingis Quair, line 158, there is an allusion to

The dromydare, the *standar oliphant*,

or the elephant that always stands.   Early naturalists
believed that the elephant had only one joint in his
legs, and so could not lie down.   When he wished to
sleep he leaned against a tree.

The name was probably given to those who were
heavy and ungainly, or endowed with great strength.

Wolf is generally a personal name, though occasionally
as in Philip *le Wolf* of the Writs of Parliament it may
be a nickname.

The name *Best* though sometimes complimentary is
generally for M. English *beste*, meaning beast.   This
meaning, happily for the present day bearers of the
name, is disguised by the spelling.

The surnames from birds are very numerous.   From
the starling, the Mid. English name of which was *stare*
come the familiar names *Starr*, *Starling* and *Stares*.

In the surname period the Mid. English name for
the Heron or Hern was *heroun* or *hern* from Old French
hairon.   From these we have the surnames *Heron* and
Hearne.

The surnames *Woodall*, *Woodwall* and *Woodwell* are
all variations of the Mid. English name *wodewele* which
stands for the woodpecker.   But this bird was also
known by several provincial names like *Wood-spite*,
Woodspack, wood-sprite.   In Smythe-Palmer's *Folk
Etymology*, p. 447, there is a quotation from Sylvester,
Du Bartas :

Eve walking forth about the Forrests, gathers
Speights, Parrots, Peacocks, Ostrich scattered feathers.

Florio has also the definition : *Picchio*, a wood-
pecker, a tree jobber, a hickway, a jobber, a *spight*.
From these dialect terms the surnames *Speight*,
Speke and *Pick* are derived.

Among well attested bird surnames we find *Crane*
(le Crane), *Crow* (*Crowe*), *Cuckoo* (*Cuckow*, Cuckowe),
Lark (le Laverock and Larke), *Woodlark* (Wodelark),
Cock (*le Koc* and *le Cok*), *Cockerell* (Cockerel and
Quoquerell), *Capon* (*le Capon* and *Capun*), *Chicken*
(*Chikin*), *Goose* (*le Gows* and *le Gos*), *Gander* (*Gandre*),
Gull (*le Gul*), *Bulfinch* (*Bolfynch*), *Finch* (*Finch* and
Fynch), *Stork* (*Storck*), *Nightingale* (*Nitingal*, *Nighte-
gale*), *Swan* (*le Swan* and *le Swon*), *Sheldrake* (*Sheldrake*
and *Sceyldrake*).

Parrot is sometimes a bird nickname, but it is also
personal from *pierrot*.

The surname *Tassell* is taken from the name of a
male hawk which is called a Tercel from Mid. Eng.
tercel, Old French *tercel, tiercel*. Cotgrave says " the
tassell or male of any kind of hawke ; so tearmed
because he is commonly a third part lesse than the
female." Another reason given is that every third
bird hatched was, in popular opinion, sure to be a male.

In " Romeo and Juliet " the heroine sighs

> For a faulconer's voice
> To lure this tassel-gentle back again,

and in Spenser's *Faerie Queen*, III, iv, 49, is another
allusion :

> Having farre off espyde a Tassel-gent,
> Which after her his nimble winges doth straine.

Buzzard is from Mid. Eng. *bosard* or *busard*, an inferior kind of falcon.

From M. English *pottoc* or *puttok*, a kite, hawk, comes the surname *Puttock*.

Associated with bird nicknames is the name *Callow*, from the Mid. English *caln, calewe*, Anglo-Saxon *caln*, meaning bald or unfledged. The word is of Latin origin.

In nicknames taken from fish we come to a much smaller class than the groups that include beasts and birds. But though these names may not be very numerous they make a respectable show in the Directories, and what they lack in variety they make up in number. Thus the general term *Fish* has given us one of our commonest surnames and the *le Fysches* and *Fishes* of the records have given their names to multitudes in succeeding generations. *Fiske* has also enjoyed a certain measure of popularity. To turn from the general we find the names John Sturgeon (Rolls of Parliament), *Whale*—popularised by the story of Jonah—in the entry Ralph *le Wal* (Hundred Rolls). To Canon Bardsley belongs the credit of discovering the curious surname *Whalebelly*, which was borne by people who had obviously done nothing to deserve so vulgar an appellation.

In City Letter Book H the name of William *Sturgeon* appears as Master of the Mistery of Pouchmakers.

A more recent announcement is that of the engagement of a Miss *Brill* which appears in the *Evening Standard* of August 6th, 1930.

The names of Thomas *Codde* and Alan *Codling* are recorded in Bromefield's *History of Norfolk*.

Turbot is a contraction of a personal Anglo-Saxon name. Nor is *Salmon* a fish nickname. It is a contracted form of the personal name *Salamon*. In the City Letter Book just quoted it is recorded that *Salamon Salamon*, a mercer, had caused unwholesome fish to be stored in a cellar near to the " Herber " (the tenement known as " Cold Harbour "). This use of the same names for font and surname is not uncommon today, especially in Welsh nomenclature, as we find such conjunctions as *David Davids, Griffith Griffiths*.

The following names are also recorded : *Trout, Gudgeon, Makarel* (Hundred Rolls), *Greyling* (*Plac. de Quo. Warranto*), *Tench* (Hundred Rolls) and Pickerel (Hundred Rolls).

NICKNAMES FROM FIELD AND LARDER

Although the principal cereals, Wheat, Rye, Oats and Barley are found among surnames, they have rarely, if ever, been given as nicknames. *Wheat* has already been dealt with. *Rye* and *Barley* are local. *Oates* is personal from Otto. But *Corn* and its compound *Barleycorn* belong to the class with which we are dealing. The name *Peppercorn* is in the Hundred Rolls.

Other cereal nicknames are *Dredge* and *Drage*, a mixed crop was known as *dredge* (Mid. English *drage*) from Old French *dragée*, mixed corn.

Peppercorn has been mentioned as a nickname surname. Its simplex *Pepper* also belongs to the same class. *Peever* is from Old French *peyvre*.

The Writs of Parliament has the name *Gingiore* for *Ginger*, from M. English *ginger*, *gingeuere*, Old French *gengibra*.

The older form of *Garlick* is recorded by Brouvefield as *Garlek*. The surname *Mustard* is rare in old records, though the entries of names like *Mustarder*, *Mustardman* and *Mustardmaker* are plentiful. The first two of these are in the Hundred Rolls. As these names are now obsolete it seems probable that some of their early possessors dropped the suffixes *er*, *man* and *maker*, leaving the simpler name *Mustard*.

Fennell from M. English *fenel* is generally a nickname. This plant was regarded by Early English and Tudor writers as an emblem of flattery. " How this smells of fennel," B. Jonson, *Case is Altered*, 1, 2.

Camomile and *Rue* are surnames from nicknames, though *rue* as the French for street must often be local, as in *De la Rue*.

Camomile or *Chamomile* is from a Greek word that we get through the late Latin *camomilla* (chamomilla) —Gr. χαμαίμηλον, lit. ground apple. Skeat suggests that this name was acquired from the apple-like smell of the flower.

It is not difficult to understand how rue became a surname, for its properties were known to all in Medieval days, and early writers have many allusions to it. Cotgrave gives the definition " Rue : Rue, Hearbe grace." In Lyte's *Herball*, p. 294, ed. 1595, Rue or Herbe Grace is described, and it is explained that as to rue is to repent, rue has been named " herb of grace " or " herb-grace." To the modern reader this plant is associated with many passages in Shakespeare, notable among which is Ophelia's speech when crazed with grief :

> "There's rue for you ; and here's some for me ; we may call it herb of grace o' Sundays : O, you must wear your rue with a difference."

Trees are generally local, but what are we to make of branch ? It may refer to a branch o' the road, but it probably indicates, in some instances, some definite spot where a branch of a tree forms a landmark as in the name of Johanna *de Branche* of the Hundred Rolls. But *Branch* is also sometimes a nickname as in Thomas Braunche of the Close Rolls.

PHRASE NICKNAMES

In the early years of the surname period the nicknamer was new to his art and contented himself by calling his victims such names as *Pike, Shanks, Foot, Thumb* or *Oliphant*. If he wished to be descriptive he used adjectives like *Fatt, Callow, Fulhardy, Sad* and *Sly*. But with practice he grew bolder and took more ambitious flights. The result of his imaginative efforts we see in what is known as the phrase-name. Like his fellow-labourers in France, Germany and Italy he succeeded to admiration. What his efforts lack in elegance they more than make up in vigour and directness, and our only regret is that some of the choicer examples of the medieval phrase-maker's art have not survived into our own time, for they would certainly have helped to revitalise a generation bored to stupefaction by the slogans of advertisement copy writers.

In Nicholl's *History of Leicestershire* appears the
name William *Badneighbour*, which is unmistakable in
meaning, but the name Simon *Badman* of the Hundred
Rolls is occupative and refers to the bidman or bedeman
who recited aves and paternosters as directed by his
patrons.

The name William *Blackinthemouth* is mentioned in
Riley's *Memorials*, but as the poet remarked about
the Heathen Chinee we are somewhat uncertain as to
what " that name might imply."

Alicia *Blisswench* was obviously one of those ladies
whom the French call " daughters of joy."

Bonenfant is the French equivalent of *Goodchild*. It
is cited in the Hundred Rolls. *Bonnyfant* is a contracted form of the name which has now become
Bullivant and *Pillivant*.

Then we find names kindred to that of William
Shakespeare in *Wagspere*, *Waghorn*, *Shakeshaft* and
Breakspear. The last of these is recorded in Clutter-
buck's *History of Hertfordshire*.

Knave is a word that has gone down in the world.
In these days it means a rogue. In the surname
period it was a common name for a servant. So
that *Brownknave* is descriptive and possibly refers to
the dress or livery. *Goodknave* is a permanent testi-
monial.

Robert *Bruselance* (Hundred Rolls) like Adrian
Breakspear evidently was careless in handling his
weapons, while John *Bukelboots* got his name through
his strange taste in what shoemakers now call " foot-
wear." In Nicholas *Buxskin* (Buckskin) recorded in

Writs of Parliament, the nicknamer again strikes the note of fashion.

Robert *Calvesmawe* (*Calvesmaghe*), a name which appears in the Writs of Parliament, has, needless to say, long been obsolete.

Catchhare, Hugh *Cachehare*, is occupative and means hunter, it is from O. Picard *cachier*, variant of O. French *chacier*, to hunt, hence to catch. Names like this beginning with a verb are common. *Catchlove* makes no appeal to tender emotions. It means Hunt Wolf.

Catchpeny, in the Hundred Rolls *Kachepeny*, doubtless refers to the enterprising habits of some medieval financier.

Cats-nose and *Cheese-and-Bread*, the last of which occurs in Knight's *Fees* have been referred to in another chapter.

The Hundred Rolls records Roger *Clenegrise* (Clean-hog). The names *Cleanhous*, *Cleanwater* and *Cleanhog* are also in evidence. *Cockesbrayne* (*Cocksbrain*) and *Cocksheved* (*Cockshead*) are triumphs of the nicknamer's art. *Cocksheved* still survives as *Coxhead*.

The Hundred Rolls also contains the name of Thomas *Cors-de-boef*. In other records the name appears as *Cor-de-beofe* and *Cordebeof* (bull-bodied).

Other curious names are *Crookbone*, *Crookhorn*, *Curtvalor*, *Derelove* (*Dearlove*), *Dent-de-fer* (*Irontooth*), and *Departe-dieu* (In God's name).

The last of these, *Departe-dieu*, is an expression that occurs three times in Chaucer's works. In *Man of Law*, Group B, l. 39, is the line :

> " Hoste " quod he, " *depardieux* ich assente."

Cotgrave under *par* gives : " De par Dieu soit, a God's name be it." Commenting on this Skeat observes " *De par* is a corruption of O. Fr. *de part*, on the part or side of."

The above may be compared with *John Dieu-te-aide*, of the Writs of Parliament.

We return to English forms in the names *Drawespe*, *Drawlace*, *Drawsword*, *Draw-water*, *Drink-ale*, *Drink-dregs*, *Drinkwater* and *Drybread*.

The Hundred Rolls records Thomas *Farewell* (Farewell) and *Feelgood*.

The Writs of Parliament has Farderless (Fatherless) and *Front-de-Bœuf* (bull-face). The French equivalent to *Farewell* is *Adieu*, this is recorded in Writs of Parliament.

Other old names are Robert *Go-before* (Rolls of Parliament), *Godsalve* (Bromfield's *Norfolk*), *Godsname* (Riley's *Memorials*), *Godthank* (Hundred Rolls), *Go-in-the-Wind* (Riley), *Good-ale-house* (Testa-Ebor), *Godisped* (*Goodspeed*), Hundred Rolls, and in this last record there is also an entry John *Gotebedde* (*Gotobed*). Strange to say *Gotobed* still survives as a surname.

Gotokirk, also in the Hundred Rolls, is a similar formation, and a name that does more honour to its bearer, seems to have disappeared.

Adam de *Halfenaked*. This name suggests a pioneer of modern fashions, but the preposition before the surname shows that the origin of the name is local. The name appears with the intrusive *de* in the Rolls of Parliament as well as the Writs. William *Handeshakere* (*Handshaker*) also in the Writs of

Parliament indicates an individual demonstrative and friendly.

Hoggesflesh as a surname sounds ungracious ; while *Holy-water-clerk* has not been terse enough for the hungry generations that have trodden down and clipped so many names that they are now almost beyond recognition.

Ironpurse. Robert *Ironpurse* (Hundred Rolls) was evidently one of those pessimists who made doubly sure of his valuables and carried them about in a portable safe.

Keepguest. The name *Kepegest* (Hundred Rolls) has a friendly sound and may have been given to some shrewd and friendly innkeeper who made his guests comfortable.

Lapwater, Henry *Lapewater* (Riley's *Memorials*), a name given to one who possibly had no interest in the carousals of his acquaintances.

John *Leve-today* (Hundred Rolls) suggests a bird of passage, *Losewit* a mental calamity and *Makeblithe* a jovial companion.

Hugh Makefere (Hundred Rolls) must have been unpleasant to meet, while everybody would welcome *Make-joy*.

Maniword (Manyword). The first owner of this name possibly aspired to fame as a politician.

The *Mucklebone* and *Mucklemans* of the Hundred Rolls had ancestors great in girth and limb.

The modern names *Pardew*, *Pardie* and *Pardoe* are from the oath *par dieu* represented in the Rolls of Parliament by John *Pardieu*.

In the Hundred Rolls appear the names of William *Peckebene*, *Alice Peckechese* and Ralph *Peckewether*, all of which point to the wearer's fondness for certain kinds of food.

Pennefather was a popular name for a miser in Medieval times and the surname is well represented in ancient documents. We find it as *Penifader*, *Pennfadir* and *Penyfader*. The version in the Hundred Rolls is *Penifadir*. The modern forms are *Pennefather* and *Pennyfather*.

Petitjean is the French equivalent of *Littlejohn*, just as *Pettitt* is of *Small* (Robert le Small, Hundred Rolls). The French adjective petit is also the first element in several of our compound surnames, as in *Petitsire*, *Petitpas*, *Petyclerk*.

Three notable names recorded in the Writs of Parliament are Reyner *Piggesflesh*, John *Pourfisshe* (Poorfish) and Peter *Pricktoe*. The phrasemongers who made up these verbal bouquets probably never imagined that they would be inscribed in State documents by solemn clerks, and preserved like flies in amber for the wonder and admiration of historians five hundred years afterwards. The second of these names, *Poorfish*, sounds like modern American slang.

The names *Rattilbagge*, *Skatergoode* (*Scattergood*), *Schorchebef* (*Scorchbeef*), *Scrothose* (*Scratchhose*), *Scutelmulh* (*Scutelmouth*), *Shoheggere* (*Shoebeggar*), *Smalewriter* (*Smallwriter*), *Sour-ale*, *Spekelitel* (Speaklittle), *Spendlove*, *Spillewyn* (Spillwine), *Sprenhose* (Spurnhose). Here we have a mixed class. One or two are quite unobjectionable. Some offer good-natured criticism. Others are mildly contemptuous. But all have definite meaning, and are not, like some names, apparent jumbles of letters that only serve the purpose of identifying their owners. Most of these, like many cited above, are now obsolete.

Many more names of this class might be given, but no useful purpose would be served by doing so, for the majority have long since passed out of existence and offer no connecting link with the obscure past that gave them birth. But to the historian and student of words they are of abiding interest. Their unstudied picturesqueness and vigour compel attention and serve in some measure to illustrate the moods and temper of a people of whom we know but little, and many of the words that form these names were, as the old Rolls show, in common use two or three centuries before they appeared in literature. The Hundred Rolls from which so many names in this book have been quoted, was compiled in 1273, more than a century before Chaucer wrote *The Canterbury Tales* and *The Vision of Piers Plowman* was completed. Until Caxton's splendid enterprise quickened the rate of literary output the only record of many English words were to be found in old Rolls and other State and municipal documents.

To the student of words the examination of the old Rolls is always an exciting adventure, and generally he finds very good sport. The descriptive adjectival names are seldom lacking in interest but the real " finds " are the descriptive compounds and phrase names. They are quaint, whimsical and archaic by turns. Some we fail to appreciate because we lack knowledge of the individuals to whom they were applied as nicknames. But for the same reason they fascinate and compel our attention. Why one lady was called *Strange-woman* and another *Termeday* we can never know. *Godsire* or *Goudsyre* (*Godfather*), *Lenechild* (*Leanchild*), *Truebody* and *Youngservant* present no difficulties. *Walkelate* hints suspicion as to character and conduct. *Strict-man* and *Wrangservice* suggest the names of characters in Tudor plays, and it is more than possible that their owners earned them by acting in the old Moralities.

Warde-dieu is a motto name, and Nicholas Goddessone, the name of a London alderman in the fourteenth century, sounds like an oath.

Two-year-old must have received his surname in infancy and Whitsuntide was evidently an important period to the person who received the surname *Whitsunday*. *Would-have* must have been grasping and the Londoner *Goldryng* was possibly so called because he was prosperous and owned this piece of jewellery. The name *Clapschethe* may have been applied to a blustering quarrelsome fellow, addicted to theatrical gestures, but who had no more stomach for a fight than the Duke of Plaza Toro, of whom W. S. Gilbert tells us that he

> Led his regiment from behind.
> He found it less exciting.

CHAPTER XII

FOREIGN NAMES

IT was the boast of our Victorian grandfathers, whom the present generation so heartily despise, that in their time Great Britain was supreme in trade and commerce. There was abundant record for the boast. Britain had then no rivals in the commercial and industrial world. Her products were the results of skill and honest workmanship and were eagerly bought everywhere and anywhere. England was the workshop of the world. Politicians, who loved to give their constituents encouraging pats on the back, were never tired of reminding them of this, and manufacturers and craftsmen glowed with modest pride as they listened to these tributes to their enterprise and skill.

The elation of these sturdy traders in their achievements was pardonable. Had they known anything about the industrial history of their country they would have entertained a wholesome respect for the foreigners within their gate, who have contributed so greatly to England's wealth and manufacturing power. For as Samuel Smile says in the first page of his book on *The Huguenots*, " England's first teachers in nearly every branch of industry were foreigners."

For centuries after the Norman Conquest, the English Channel—that great natural defence—saved Britain from the intermittent warfare that prevailed everywhere throughout Europe.   In its sheltered position England became a great grazing country and the wool and fells of its sheep were the foundation of the national wealth. But as neither Saxon or Norman knew anything about manufacture the wool was sold to French and Flemish weavers who made it into cloth.

But the Norman and Plantagenet Kings saw that, profitable as this arrangement was, the English traders were paying a heavy price for their lack of technical skill.   " The ribs of all nations throughout the world," were as Matthew Paris said, " kept warm by the fleeces of English wool," but the profits of the dyeing and weaving of these fleeces went into the pockets of foreigners. They sent out invitations to Flemish artisans to settle in England, offering abundant wages and special privileges.   These offers were accepted, and as the Low Countries were often disturbed by civil war and the feuds of the local Guilds, the tide of immigration rose steadily and the Flemish colonies in England grew in number and importance.

One of the first of these was established at Worsted, near Norwich, in the reign of Henry I.   Through the skill and industry of this little band of immigrants the name of the little village became for ever associated with the principal product of their looms.   These colonists were also the first to use water-driven corn and fulling mills.

But though its rulers continued to show favour to foreigners who settled in England no substantial progress was made in establishing the manufacture of cloth until the reign of Edward III. This King realised even more clearly than his predecessors, that home industries needed encouragement and development. He sent a number of trusted agents to the Low Countries to invite a number of distressed Flemish weavers to come to England and teach the workpeople here the best methods of spinning, dyeing and weaving. The invitation came to the Flemings as a Heaven-sent deliverance. The year was 1338. Louis de Nevers, Count of Flanders, at the instigation of Philip de Valois of France, had ordered the arrest of all Englishmen in Flanders. With the execution of this order, war blazed up between England and France, the export of wool, and the import of cloth was prohibited by the English Government, and the weavers of the Low Countries found themselves on the brink of starvation. King Edward renewed his offer to the indigent Flemings and granted a charter for the protection of any of these foreigners who settled in London. The offer was gratefully accepted, and the Flemings flocked in large numbers to England. Among their leaders was one John *Kempe* to whom royal letters of protection were granted to carry on his trade, and " to teach it to such of our people as shall be inclined to learn it." Kempe settled in Kendal and began there to manufacture the cloth for which the picturesque little Westmoreland town is still famous.

Of other notable settlers there were *Willielmus* and *Hancheinus* de Brabant, the latter of whom is supposed to have given his name to the *hank* of worsted. These men plied their trade in York.

Nottingham was also a centre where the woollen trade was established and brought wealth to many, among whom the names of *Bugge*, *Willoughby*, *Mappurley*, *Amyas*, *Plumtre*, *Tamesley*, *Bingham* and *Hunt* are prominent.

The Bugges and Willoughbys were joint ancestors of the house of Willoughby.   There is no need to smile at the name of Bugge.   It may have an unpleasant sound to English ears, but it is a Teutonic name of long and great lineage and a contracted form of *Burghart*, castle strong.

The brothers Blanket who set up the manufacture of the colourless cloth, from which they took their name, encountered strong opposition from the magistrates of Bristol when they began to work their looms in that city.   They then appealed to the King who ordered the Corporation of the Western city " to permit the machines to be erected . . . without making on that account any reproach, hindrance or undue exaction."

The same enlightened policy was pursued by succeeding Kings.   In 1430 Henry VI invited three German engineers, Michael *Gosselyn*, George *Harbryke* and Matthew *Laweston* with thirty skilled miners to work the royal tin mines in Cornwall.

In 1565 the first wire-drawing mill was started in England by Christopher Schütz (Archer).   Needlemaking was introduced by another German.

Paper making was introduced from the Low Countries.   The first three paper mills established were failures and it was not until John *Spielmann* (musician),

Queen Elizabeth's jeweller, erected his paper mill at Dartford in 1598 that paper-making became a profitable enterprise in England.

In the reign of James I " three prime workmen " were brought from Rochelle to instruct English craftsmen in the process of manufacturing the alum used in dyeing. To ensure their safe arrival in England these three preceptors were smuggled out of France in *hogsheads*.

But the immigrations already mentioned were insignificant in comparison with those caused by religious persecutions in Germany, France and Flanders. The first of these occurred in the latter half of the sixteenth century. The next came a hundred years later. The first was of French, Flemish and German Protestants, and the second, French Huguenots. How vast these immigrations were may be judged from the following facts.

When Luther raised the standard of revolt against the Church, Flanders was at the height of its prosperity. Its chief port, Antwerp, was the commercial centre of Northern Europe, and it was not uncommon to find as many as two thousand ships at one time in the Scheldt taking in cargo. The accession of Philip II was the signal for trouble. Civil war followed, and Alva and Parma were set the task of breaking the spirit of a proud and independent race. The struggle lasted for many years, as did the flight of the Protestants. Several hundred thousands of skilled craftsmen left the country for Holland, England and Germany. Many of these who came to England established new industries.

14

A few years later followed the massacre of St. Bartholomew, in France, which in its turn was followed by civil war, and the escape of many Huguenots to England. These, like the Flemings, were enterprising traders, skilled craftsmen, experienced soldiers, and their leaders ministers of religion, doctors and lawyers. Like their neighbours from Flanders they were warmly welcomed by the English Government. Almost from the time of their arrival they were able to support themselves, and as they soon developed new trades, and manufactured wares that had previously been imported from France they were instrumental in greatly extending the wealth and power of their adopted land.

In 1685 the Revocation of the Edict of Nantes drove half a million French subjects into exile. Of these more than 100,000 settled in Great Britain and Ireland. These refugees were of all classes, and among them were distinguished scientists and philosophers, landed gentry, merchants, and many professional men.

When we remember that from the Norman Conquest the tide of immigration has never ceased to flow towards England and that the numbers of those who came in the sixteenth and seventeenth centuries were far greater than any that had come since the early Saxon settlements, it seems difficult to understand why so few foreign names are to be found in the Directories. One explanation is that when foreigners settled down in this country and formed ties, they either from choice, or because they found it more conducive to harmonious relations with their neighbours, adopted English surnames. It is true that many did this, and there is no doubt that in doing so they showed good sense. For though successive Kings adopted a benevolent attitude to these strangers, the people looked upon them with jealousy and suspicion, and as interlopers who had come to steal away their bread.

Thus, as Smiles states, there is in the parish church of Allhallows, Barking, the monument of a distinguished Fleming, Roger *Haestrecht*, who changed his name to *James*, and was the founder of the family of *James* of Igtham Court in Kent.

Then there was Henry *Hoek* or *Hook*, another Fleming, from Wesel, who was a prosperous brewer. This man adopted the name of *Leeke*.

The Goupés, who made their home in Wiltshire, modified the name to *Guppy*, and the *Thunguts* translated their name to *Dodgood*, of which there is also the variant *Teegood*.

Many of the Huguenot refugees adopted English translations of their names. So that *Le Noir* became *Black*; *Le Maur*, *Brown*; *L'Oiseau*, *Bird*; *Le Jeune*, *Young*; *Le Blanc*, *White*; *La Croix*, *Cross*; *Le Roy*, *King*; *Le Monnier*, *Miller*; *Tonnolier*, *Cooper*; *Dulau*, *Waters*; *Le Maitre*, *Masters*; *Le Fevre*, *Smith*; *Tête*, *Head*; *Boulanger*, *Baker*; *Lépine*, *Thorne*; *Frere*, *Brothers*.

Other names, as Smiles relates in *The Huguenots*, were curiously rendered. Thus the French nickname *Joli-femme* became *Pretyman*, *Planché* was anglicised as *Plank*, *Momerie* became *Mummery*, while the local name *Villebois* suffered a sea-change and became

Williamise.   Boyer became *Bower;* and *Bois, Boys* as well as Wood.   Other transformations were *Taillebois* to *Talboys, Bouchier* to *Butcher* or *Boxer, Le Coq* to *Laycock, Mesurier* to *Measure, Mahieu* to *Mayhew, Bourgeois* to *Burgess, Souverain* to *Suffren, Drouet* to *Drewitt,* and *D'Orleans* to *Darling.*

Smiles complains that the great name Condé was dreadfully vulgarised by transforming it to *Cundy.* It certainly seems a pity that a name of such historical renown should be abandoned for the name of a *conduit.* But the historian is on less certain ground when he complains of vulgarisation in the change from *De Preux* into *Diprose.* For the surname *Diprose* is from *des preaux,* meaning, of the meadows, and is one of the cases where the prefix became part of the name when it passed into English.

The surname *Shoppee* of which Smiles also complains as a rendering of *Chappuis,* is ludicrous, and does not look like an English surname. What probably happened is that when the immigrant told the Government or parish official his name the officer tried to write down the name phonetically, with the result— *Shoppee.* Had he known the meaning of the word he would have entered the name as *Carpenter,* which is the English equivalent of Old French *Chappuis.*

Nor is Smiles right in finding fault with *Mullins* as an anglicised form of *Moulins,* the French term for Mills.   The official might have entered the immigrants' name as *Molyneux* which sounds much more aristocratic but the meaning would only have been slightly modified for *Molyneux* is the diminutive of *Mullins.*

Other changes to which Smiles objected were from *Pelletier* to *Pelter* ; *Huyghens* to *Huggins* and *Higgins*, and *Beaufoy* to *Boffey*.

Dealing with the change from *Pelletier* to *Pelter*, we would first remark that in the pronunciation of long names the average Englishman is, and has always been, incurably careless and slipshod. If he can contract a word without entirely destroying its sense, he invariably does so, and the contraction of long names is almost too common to be specially noticeable. The tendency has always been to simplify and contract words. Thus we get *Beecham* from *Beauchamp*, and *Harmsworth* from *Harmondsworth*. Place names are treated in the same way. To people of the Eastern counties *Caverham* is *Canham* and *Wymondham*, *Wyndham*. Then why object to *Pelter* for *Pelletier ?*

Huggins is a personal name and a diminutive of *Hugh*.

Whoever was responsible for substituting *Boffey* for *Beaufoy* certainly made a mistake, for in this word *foy* is Old French for *beech*, and the word means beautiful or splendid beech. But *Boffey* is a contraction of *Bounefoy* or good faith, so that *Boffey* and *Beaufoy* are not related.

Modification of French names to English forms recorded by Smiles include *Letellier* to *Taylor*. Here the more appropriate name would have been *Weaver*, for *Letellier*, like the English *Teler*, means weaver, and originates from the Latin *tile*, a web. Here it is clear that the name-giver has confused the French words *Letailleur* and *Letellier*, the first of which is the French equivalent for tailor, and the second, weaver.

Brasseur also became *Brassey ; Batchelier, Bachelor ;
Pigou, Pigott ; Breton, Britton ; Dieudonné, Dudney ;
Baudoir, Baudry ; Guilbert, Gilbert ; Koch, Cox ;
Renalls, Reynolds ; Mermean, Meryon ; Saveroy,
Savery ; Gebon, Gibbon ; Scardeville, Sharwell ;* and
Levereau, Lever.

But the leaders of this great Exodus who had won
distinction in many walks of life retained the names
they had rendered famous.

The late Archbishop Trench, who did so much to
popularise the study of words, was descended on his
father's and mother's side from two notable Huguenot
families, those of *Chevenix* and *Trench*.

David *Garric*, the grandfather of the famous actor,
Garrick, fled to England from Bordeaux at the Revoca-
tion. Other names are those of *Courtauld, Delaine*,
an ancestor of *Delane*, the editor of *The Times ;
Poupart, Lobjoit, Fonblanque, Baringer, Dargan,
Martineau, Auriol, Boileau, Des Champes, Drelincourt,
Forestier* or *Forrester, Houblon, Layard, La Fanu,
Ligonier, Olier, D'Olyer* now *Hollyer, Unwin* or *Onwhyn*,
and *Vanbrugh*.

Though in this list only a few names of distinguished
refugees are given, we cannot close it without mention-
ing that eminent scholar *Casaubon*, who came and
settled in England after the assassination of Henry IV
of France. There were also Solomon de *Caux* or *Caus*,
one of the first inventors of the steam-engine ; *Constant*,
who took service under the Prince of Orange ; *Cottereau*
the famous horticulturist ; *Du Brosses*, one of whose
descendants took the name of *Bros*, and was secretary

of the Bank of England ; Tom *Durfey*, the song writer
and dramatist ; George *Jeune*, ancestor of Dr. Jeune,
Dean of Jersey ; David *Kerk*, the celebrated seaman ;
Elie *Palairet*, author and preacher ; *Puget*, who founded
the foreign banking house of Puget, Bambridge & Co.
in Saint Paul's Churchyard, London ; and James
Rousseau, the landscape painter.

Other French surnames that have found asylum in
English Directories are the personal names *André*,
Armand and *Benoit*. André is the French equivalent
of Andrew and *Benoit* of Benedict. *Armand* corres-
ponds to the English Harman and is from Old German
Hariman, Anglo-Saxon *Hereman*.

From the Latin *Augustin*, augustinus, majestic, the
German name *August*, the French *Auguste*, and the
English *Austin* and *Austen* are derived.

Berger, *Bergier*, shepherd, and *Bouvier* and *Boyer*,
cattle drover, are French occupative names. *Berger*
has the variant *Le berger*, and the diminutive *Bergeret*
and *Bergerot*, but these are confined to the French
Directories. The English surname corresponding to
Bouvier is *Buller*.

The French *Brun* and the Dutch *Brunel*, brown, are
colour nicknames, and Doré, the name of the imaginative French artist, means *golden*.

Other notable French nicknames are *Coquard* old,
dandy, from *coq*, a cock ; and *Callard* and *Caillard*.
In some instances these are costume nicknames and
mean piebald. In other cases the name is a bird
nickname from the French word *caille*, a quail.

An offensive example of the same type is provided

by the name *Bouchard* which stands for *big mouth*. But as with English, the biggest proportion of French surnames found in our Directories are local.

Beaufort, a fine or noble stronghold, from *beau* fine, noble and *fort*, a fortress, from Latin *bellus*, *fortis*, is a well-known French surname. *Bussy* is the French for thicket or wood and comes from Old French *buc*, O.H. German *busc*.

The name *Coudray* is French for hazel-grove, and *De Fraine* means, of the ash-tree.

Duchêne and *Duchesne* are, of the ash-tree, and *Dupont*, of the bridge. A common local name is *Langlais* or *Langlois*, the Englishman.

Du pre, *Dupre* and *Duprat* correspond to the English surnames *Dupree* and *Duppery* and mean of the meadows. *Duval* is also local for of the valley.

Farge is for the dweller at the forge and *Faudel* means sheepfold. *Fargion* is a diminutive of *Farge*.

Faure and *Favre* are occupative, from *Faber*, smith, carpenter.

Other French occupative surnames often met with in English name-lists are *Fournier*, oven keeper or baker ; *Larcher*, the archer ; *Poupart* and *Poupard*, child, youngster, from French *poupard ;* and *Royer*, wheelwright.

Equally popular are the personal names *Giraud*, the French form of Gerald ; and the two diminutives of Martin, *Martinet* and *Martineau*. As we have seen above *Martineau* was a famous Huguenot name.

The famous Flemish surname *De Wit* is a colour nickname and corresponds to the English *White*, and the equally well-known Scandinavian *Pederson* is personal and is Peder's, i.e. Peter's son. *Hendrik* (Dutch and Scand.) is equivalent to Henry.

Sperling, Sparrow ; Schwann, Swann ; Fink, Finch ; and *Falk* and *Falke, Falcon, Hawk,* are German bird nicknames.

Schiller, the name of the famous German poet and dramatist, means squinter. The nickname is from German *schieler,* a squinting person. But it must be said that some of the poet's admirers and compatriots claim that his name is from *schiller,* meaning colour play or iridescence.

As we are discussing poets it may not be inappropriate to mention the name of another German writer whose lyrics have for nearly a century charmed the world with their exquisite beauty and emotional appeal, H. *Heine.* His name is a diminutive of Heinrich.

Heinz, Heintz, is personal and the genitive of *Hein.*

The German *Gottschalk* stands for God's servant. The second element of the name is from old H. German *scalc,* servant.

The nickname *Friedmann* means man of peace, and *Seligman* blessed, or happy. The German name *Gasse,* street, is local, as are the variants *Sachs* and *Sax,* Saxon.

Schenk, wine and beer retailer, and *Lehmann,* vassal, from Old H. German *lehan,* fee, fief, are surnames quite familiar to English people. *Bauer,* peasant ; *Baumann,* builder ; *Ackermann,* farmer, from O. High German *ackar, acchar,* a field ; *Bergmann,* miner, hillman ; *Vogler,* fowler ; *Wagner,* waggoner ; *Weber,* weaver ; *Weigand,* warrior.

Schmidt, smith, is as popular in Germany as elsewhere, but compounds of the name are commoner than the simplex, as in *Goldschmidt, Silberschmidt, Kupferschmidt* (coppersmith). Germans love compounds, in names, as in other words.

The precious metals are also represented in many German compounds. Thus of *Silber* (silver) we find in the *Nat. Tele. Directory*, 1930, *Silberberg* (silver mountain), *Silberblatt* (silverleaf), *Silberman, Silbernagel* (silvernail), *Silberklang* (silversound), *Silberrad* (silverwheel), *Silberstein* (silverstone).

Gold is equally prolific, for among its compounds are *Goldacker*, the equivalent of *Goldfield*, *Goldberg* (goldhill), *Goldblatt* (goldleaf), *Goldblum* (goldflower), *Goldburg* (goldcastle), *Goldfarb* (golden colour), *Goldklang* (golden sound), *Goldschneider* (tailor), *Goldstein* (gold stone) and *Goldzweig* (goldbough).

Several of these are Jewish names and were taken a little more than a hundred years ago when the people of the ancient faith in the German States were compelled to take surnames. The wealthier and more influential Jews were permitted a certain liberty of choice, but the majority were compelled to adopt those—and many were offensive nicknames—which unsympathetic officials chose to thrust upon them. Among these were fanciful and picturesque names like *Apfelbaum* (appletree), *Rubenstein*, ruby, and flower names, as in *Rosen* (roses) and its compounds *Rosenbaum* (tree), *-berg* (hill), *-blatt* (leaf), *-blum* (flowers), *-krautz* (crown), *-dale*, *-feld* (field), *-garten* (garden), *-hain* (grove), *-heim* (home), *-stein* (stone), *-thal* (valley), and *Rosenzweig* (rose-twig).

Bach, brook, a name made illustrious by the great musical composer, frequently occurs in English Directories, as is also another local name *Steiner*, dweller by a rock.

Other German names, well known on this side of the North Sea, are *Albrecht*, Albert ; *Behrend*, bear from Old German *Berin*, diminutive form of Old H. German *bere*, beer ; *Behrens*, genitive form of above ; *Be(h)ring*, bear's son, the suffix *ing* meaning son. *Bernhardt* is also from the diminutive *Berin*.

In English we have the surnames *Seabright* and *Sebright* from the vivid Anglo-Saxon names *Sigebeorht*, and *Sæbeorht* meaning victory, bright. The corresponding German names are *Siebert* and *Sigebert*. These mean victory, glorious, from O.H. German *sigi*, victory, and *beroht*, bright, glorious. The names *Siegmund* and *Sigmund* are akin to the above and mean victorious protection, M.H. German *mund*, O.H. German *munt*, meaning protection.

As in England, colour names like *Schwartz*, black, and *Weiss*, white, are among the commonest surnames in Germany.

The Dutch names best known to English people are nearly all local, like *Vanderbilt*, of the heap ; *Vandervelde*, of the field ; *Vandyck*, of the dike ; and *Van Gelder*, of Gelderland.

Vanbrugh, the name of the witty dramatist and capable architect, is Flemish and Dutch, and means, of the bridge. A common Dutch surname, also well known to us is the animal nickname *Haas*, hare.

Kramer and *Krammer* are Dutch occupative names and were given originally to a mercer or pedlar.

De Jong is Dutch and means, the younger.

Ralli is Italian and a variant of the personal name *Rollo*, which in its turn is the equivalent of the French font name *Raoul*.

Durante is an Italian adjectival name and means enduring.

Larsen, Ohlsen and *Olsen* are Scandinavian personal names. *Larsen* is for Lar's (Lawrence's) son. *Olsen* is a variant of *Ohlsen* and means Olaf's son.

Da Silva is a Portugese local surname and translated literally means, of the wood.

The Spanish *De la Cruz* is the equivalent of the French *De la Croix*, of the cross.

These, needless to say, are but a selection of the foreign names to be found in English Directories. It is remarkable that the majority of these are German, and that the countries, France and Flanders, which have done more than any other to swell our census returns are but poorly represented. The explanation of this is that comparatively few Flemings or Frenchmen took up their residences in this country after the end of the seventeenth century. The descendents of these people after so long a residence now regard themselves as English people, and have either taken English names or so anglicised their own that they are no longer recognisable as foreign designations.

On the other hand German immigration began with the Hanoverian Kings. When George I came to England a long retinue of soldiers, noblemen, painters and musicians followed him, and spread the blessings of German culture. German traders followed, and many of their compatriots settled here, and have retained the original names which have long been associated with honourable enterprise. But the name changing process continues, and in process of time great Teutonic names that recall the heroic deeds of ancient warriors, will be changed for those of Smith or Brown.

CHAPTER XIII

CRAFTSMEN AND OFFICIALS

> For this ilond is beest and bringeth forth trees and
> fruyt and oxen and other bestes, and wyn groweth there
> in some place. The lond hath plante of foules and of
> bestes of dyvers manere kynde, the lond is plenteuous
> and the see also. . . . Therefore a versifioure in
> his metre preyseth the lond in this manere, Engelond
> ful of play, fremen well worthy to pleye ; fre men,
> fre tonges, hert fre ; free heelth al the leden (folk) ;
> here (their) lond is more fre, more better than here
> (their) tonge.—JOHN DE TREVISA (1326-1402).

THE more we study the literature of the surname period
and the early Rolls in which the names of the forefathers
of our race are recorded, the more we realise how wide
and deep is the gulf that separates us from that distant
period. The difference between the medieval Englishman and his descendants is as great as that between the
modern Briton and the Hottentot. In no particular
is that difference more strongly marked than in the
commercial and industrial systems of the two periods.

It is true that there are points of resemblance. The
Merchant Guild has been replaced by the Combine and
Trust, and the Trades Unions function in the place of
the Craftsmen's Guild, and the new organisations pay
as little regard to the needs of a long suffering public
as did their ancestors. And in one or two of the ancient
trades there is little change, except in method. The

gardener still uses spade and shears. The ploughman
drives his furrow as in the days of Virgil, but his plough
is now drawn by horses instead of oxen.

But with these and other exceptions, trade and
industry has been subject to many changes since the
fourteenth century.

If we turn to the Order of the Pageant of the Play of
Corpus Christi at York in 1415 we find a list of trades
carried on at that time in the ancient northern city,
with the order in which the representatives of these
trades walked in procession. Some of these trades
like those of the Armourers, Water Leaders, Bowers
and Fletchers have long since disappeared. The
Penniger no longer proudly bears aloft the ensign of
the Lord whose retainer he is. But though his office
is abolished the surname which has weathered the
changes of half a thousand years serves to remind us
of its dignity and importance. A similar fate has
overtaken the Scottish *Bannermann* who performed
the same duties, and the surname to which this calling
gave birth has been borne by a Prime Minister, who
refused to abandon it for a title.

Another retainer of some importance was the
sensechal (Mid. Latin *siniscaleus*, *famulorum senior*, the
steward). The holder of this situation has given us
two surnames. In the Rolls of Parliament we find
William *le Seneschal*. Its modern equivalent is
Senechal. The name is of Gothic origin and is from
Gothic *sineigs*, old, and *Skalks*, a servant. The second
element in this name is also found in the surname
Gottschalk, God's servant. The office of marshal

became one of high honour, and under the Angevin Kings the marshals were the most responsible officers in the Royal household and exercised great power. But in its beginnings these servants were among the humblest, as we find from the derivation of the word. This is from O. High German mähre (Eng. mere), horse, and *schalk*, a servant. Cp. French *mareschal*, a blacksmith.

The names Miles *le Speller* of the Close Rolls, and Gerald *le Spiller* of the Rolls of Parliament remind us that in those far off days there were orators and spell-binders. The Duke of Wellington once remarked to a famous Diarist that in his position as Chancellor of an ancient University he was much *exposed* to authors. But the lords and knights who met in great assemblies had little to fear from the outpourings of the orators, for their efforts were confined to the readings of addresses and proclamations, and in no way resembled the masterpieces of the modern soap-box rhetoricians. The name is from Old. Eng. *spell*, a discourse.

Among household officers we find Robert *le Panter* (Hundred Rolls), Nicholas *le Suur* (*Sewer*), Hundred Rolls, Adam *le Karver* (*Carver*), Hundred Rolls, and *John le Page*, Writs of Parliament. It would be unprofitable to discuss the various duties to each of the many servants of a great household in the fourteenth century, though they are minutely set out by French and Italian medieval writers. It is enough for present purposes to state that the *Panter* was in charge of the *Bread*, i.e. food; the *Sewer* served the food, and according to an ancient book on *Carving*, conveyed

" all manner of pottages, metes and sauces "; the carver fulfilled the duties that his name suggests. The *Page* stood behind his lord at table and held his cup. As forks were then unknown, the etiquette of the period demanded that no one at table should set on fish, flesh or fowl more than two fingers and a thumb.

But to the fastidious even this restricted use of the fingers must have rendered the services of the *Ewer* and *Napper* indispensable. The first of these brought water in a bowl or ewer, the second a napkin, so that those who had dined could wash their hands. These servants also took surnames from their occupations and we find those as Richard *le Ewere* (Rolls of Parliament) and John *le Naper* (Hundred Rolls) and Jordan *le Nappere*. To these old names the present-day *Ewers*, *Nappers* and *Napiers* owe their surnames.

As England first became prosperous through herds and flocks, the herdsman who tended those flocks was, to use the argot of modern commerce, the " keyman " of the industry. Unless he tended his charges with care and skill all else was unavailing. The name is generally found in compounds which showed the kind of herd he tended, but the simplex herd has afforded a surname which in the Hundred Rolls figures as John *le Hirde*.

As befitting England's principal industry there was much sub-division of labour. Of this our surnames supply abundant evidence, for among them we find *Shepherd*, *Oxherd* (John *Oxenhyrde*, Peter *Oxhird*), *Calvehird*, William *le Kuherde* and Adam *le Cowhirde*, *Stothird* and *Stolherd*, *Coulthirde* and *Cowthird*, *Weatherherd*, *Gottard*, *Swinhird*, *Sowhard*, *Hogherder*, *Swonherde*,

15

Gusehyrd. These names are taken from the Hundred Rolls, the Durham Household Book, Testiam. Ebor, Writs of Parliament, Wills and Inventories, York, Valor Ecclesiasticus and Corpus Christi Guild.

This is not a complete list of the hirds, but it is sufficiently comprehensive to show the wide ramifications of the grazing industry. The Shepherd or Sheepherd's name remains to us unchanged. *Oxherd* is now obsolete. *Calvehird* has assumed the more graceful form of *Calvert*. *Kuherde* and *Cowhirde* has developed into the unpleasant sounding *Coward*. *Stothird* and *Stothard* have become *Stotherd*, *Stoddard* and *Stoddart*. *Colthirde* and *Cowthird* have become *Coultart*, *Coulthard* and *Coultherd*. *Weatherherd* has been corrupted to *Weatherhead*, and *Gottard* has assumed the simpler form of *Goddard*. *Swynhird* is now *Swinnart ; Hogherde*, *Hoggart ;* and *Swonherde*, *Swanherde*, though the last name is now very rare. *Gushyrde* is now met with as *Gooseherd*.

Some of these animal names are compounded with *man* instead of *hird* as in *Cowman* and *Coltman*. Both *Cowhird* and *Cowman* were servants but the work they did was different. There are many occupative compounds ending in *man*. To take only a few there are *Palfreyman* as well as *Coltman* and *Runciman*, *Bullman* as well as *Cowman*, and in this group we also find *Heiferman*, *Pigman*, *Sowman* and *Hogman*. *Priestman* and *Monkman* mean servant of the priest or monk. Sometimes man appears in Anglo-Saxon personal names as in *Rickman* from *Ricman*, and *Walkman* from *Wealhman*.

To return to occupative names the old records contain such names as *Couchmen, Coachman, Coacheman, Charman, Carman, Wainman* or *Wenman*. The *Bridgeman*, as explained in a former chapter, was in charge of, or collected, tolls at the bridge. The *Yeatman* guarded the gate. The *Parkman, Moorman* and *Pullman* had duties in connection with the park, the moor and the pool. *Vickerman* like *Priestman* was the vicar's servant. *Wudeman* possibly sometimes represented the woodcutter or hunter, but it was also an Anglo-Saxon personal name. Harrison in his *Dictionary of Surnames* mentions a proclamation issued by the Queen of Edward the Confessor, in which she asked for judgment against an undesirable tenant named *Woodeman* who had paid no rent, and borrowed a horse two years before which he had not returned. The *Chapman* we are already familiar with. But there were also those smaller dealers, the wandering salesmen known as the *Copeman* and the *Packman*. Some devote their energies to the sale of one commodity like the *Cheasman* who retailed cheese, the *Wadman*, the *Capman, the Coulman* and the *Riceman*.

Sometimes the compound with *man* is the shortened form of a place name as in *Lakeman* for *Lakenham*. Very often it is a nickname as in *Kinsman, Nedyman, Youngman, Oldman, Smallman, Strongman, Longman, Lyteman, Quarterman* or *Quartermain, Trotman, Prettiman, Whiteman, Blackman, Hendiman, Sweetman, Proudman, Goodman*. There are also the local names, *Ruddiman*, who lived at the *Rood*, the *Crouchman* at the cross, the *Meatman* at the mead, the *Steadman* at the stead, the *Knapman* on the hill or knap, the *Holman* at the holm, the *Knowlman* at the knoll, the *Hatchman* at the hatch, and *Sellerman*, at or in the cellar.

But the principal suffix denoting trade or occupation was *er* and *ier* with the feminine *ster*. These, as in French and German, had replaced the Teutonic *a-* which is found in the Anglo-Saxon, *wyrht-a*, wright. Just as in German we have *Fischer*, fisher and *Hausmeier*, housesteward, so a very considerable proportion of English occupative surnames have the *er* or *ier* ending.

Of these very many examples might be given, but perhaps the use of the suffix is best illustrated in the following extract from *Cocke Lorelle's Bote*, a rather wearisome piece of doggerel that appeared early in the sixteenth century. This includes the names of many of the London traders and craftsmen of the period.

> The fyrst was goldesmythes and grote clyppers :
> Multyplyers and clothe thyckers :
> Called fullers everychone :
> There is taylers, taverners, and drapers :
> Potycaryes, ale-brewers and bakers :
> Mercers, fletchers, and sporyers :
> Boke-prynters, peynters, bowers :
> Myllers, carters, and botylemakers :
> Owchers, skynners, and cutlers :
> Bladesmythes, fosters, and sadelers :
> Coryers, cordwayners, and cobelers :
> Gyrdelers, forborers, and webbers :
> Sponers, torners and hatters :
> Lynewebbers, setters with lyne-drapers :
> Roke-makers, copersmythes, and lorymers :
> Brydel-bytlers, blackesmythes, and ferrars :

There are many verses more in this strain, but there is no good reason for troubling the reader with any more of it.

But though these verses may not be poetry they have some interest for the student.   For they point to one of the main sources of our surnames.   Most of the trade names in *Cocke Lorelle's Bote*, and there are hundreds of them, have furnished us with them. Some readers who boast a more ancient lineage may be disturbed at the thought that they take their name from some medieval tradesman.   But let them take comfort in the reflection that though John Bull has stood behind the shop counter for many generations and is known to all as one in no way ashamed to soil his hands with business, he has ever held his head high among the nations.   The wealth and power which commerce has given us have proved priceless assets in days of national crisis, and those who have helped in any way to create that wealth have no cause to resent the thought of having done such honourable service.

CHAPTER XIV

Teutonic Surnames

Verse was a necessary medium of knowledge, and the poet an essential officer of the State. All the historical monuments of the north are full of the honours paid this order of men both by princes and peoples ; nor can the annals of poetry produce any age or country which reflects more glory and lustre upon it. The ancient chronicles constantly represent the Kings of Denmark, Norway and Sweden as attended by one or more Skalds ; for this was the name they gave their poets. They were more especially honoured and caressed at the courts of those princes who distinguished themselves by their great actions and passion for glory.— *Northern Antiquities*, Trans. from the French of M. Mallet by Bishop Percy (Bohn, 1859).

For a long period after the fall of the Roman Empire, the Northmen scourged Europe with fire and sword. Of peaceful pursuits they knew little and cared less. War was their profession and they lived by plunder.

While he reigned, Charlemagne held them in check, but none could crush them, and the successors of that great monarch offered them only the feeblest resistance. They gloried in feats of arms, and would brook no interference with their liberty from any ruler, however mighty. To them cowardice and tyranny were the only vices, and the sole virtue valour. To die with his arms in his hand was the vow of every soldier ; while every man who had done some worthy deed in battle was accorded the honours due to a hero. These exploits were also commemorated in odes that were passed from minstrel to minstrel and sung or chanted at all public festivals or ceremonies.

The Northmen were as formidable on sea as land, and their expeditions ranged from Constantinople to the coast of Portugal. Many times in the course of two centuries they made descents upon England, Scotland, Ireland, Courland, Levonia; all suffered from their depredations. They spread over Holland and Flanders and Lower Saxony. They harried the French coasts; their ships sailed up all the French rivers, and as M. Mallet has told us, in the space of thirty years frequently burnt and pillaged Paris and all the principal towns and cities of France. Greece, Italy and Spain also suffered from their depredations.

But the most remarkable of these raids was that undertaken by Ralph or Rollo, a descendant, it is said, of the ancient Kings of Norway. For this voyage was linked up with the future destiny of England. Banished from Norway by King Harold, Rollo first sailed for the Hebrides where he was joyfully received by a number of Norwegian nobles, who had fled there for refuge. These nobles elected Rollo as their chief and asked nothing better than to share in any enterprise he might undertake.

As he had now a considerable force at his command and many ships of war, Rollo determined to strike a blow at England. But here he had to deal with Alfred the Great who was not so weak and acquiescent as previous English rulers. Rollo made several attempts to establish a settlement in England but each of these efforts were frustrated by the energy and watchfulness of the Saxon King. Finding his attempts to gain a footing in England of no avail Rollo headed his ships for France. There he met with immediate success. He sailed up the Seine to Rouen, then the capital of the province known as Neustria. Making this his base of operations he continued his voyage up the river, and laid siege to Paris. His operations were so successful that in a short time Charles the Simple bought off the invaders by ceding to them the province of Neustria. Rollo received it in perpetuity to himself and his posterity as a feudal duchy dependent on the crown of France. This statement has been disputed by modern historians who aver that Rollo went to St. Clair, gave his hand to the King in token that he wished to live at peace with the Franks, and that Charles was doubtless only too glad to accept these conditions. But whatever the conditions, Rollo or Raoul I became possessor of the Duchy, afterwards called Normandy, and governed it with such wisdom and moderation that in a few years it became one of the finest provinces of Europe.

Rollo and his followers embraced Christianity, but their adoption of the new faith in no way lessened their martial ardour. They chose St. Michael as their patron saint and under his banner hastened to Southern Italy then the favourite battle ground of Lombards, Germans and Saracens. In 1029 they took possession of Aversa. A few years later the sons of Tancred de Hauteville became rulers of Apulia. Finally Robert Guscard drove the Saracens from Sicily, and he and his fellow Normans thus became masters of Southern Italy.

In that latter part of the eleventh century the Normans were masters of more than half of Europe. William the Conqueror sat on the English throne. Henry IV ruled Germany. The Cid was master of Spain, and Robert Guscard of the South of Italy. Hildebrand sat in the Papal chair, and a century of Norman achievement was fittingly crowned when Godfrey de Bouillon planted the banner of the Crusaders on the walls of Jerusalem.

From this rapid historical sketch the sources of many of our words and names become apparent. The descendents of Rollo who invaded England though they had adopted the language of the duchy they had occupied retained many of their ancestral names. Other Frenchmen who followed them to England brought with them the names they had inherited from Frankish invaders. Nor should we forget that in addition to the early Saxon immigrants considerable stretches of the country had been occupied by Danish and Norwegian settlers, and that it was a Danish king who made England a kingdom.

Had all the names from these many sources survived the result would have been inextricable confusion. But happily for the peace of mind of philological students many of them passed out of use after the Norman Conquest. Of those that remained a part were kept alive by the peasantry—ever the last refuge of conservatism—possibly as a reminder of older and happier times. The rest were names which the

Norman favoured, for various reasons. Many of the former appear in old records in Latinised forms, very difficult to recognise. Others have a French form, while some are modified forms of Saxon names. So that in some cases we find both the English and French forms of the same Teutonic surname.

Thousands of Anglo-Saxon names still survive, as well as a considerable number of Teutonic origin that were introduced by the French, and are from Germanic sources. Many of these are older than recorded history and carry us back to the days of legend and fable, when the boldest Vikings spoke the name of Odin in hushed accents, and the demi-gods that dwelt among the mists of Asgard inspired heroes of commoner clay to daring adventure and noble deed.

These Teutonic names have found a place in several European languages, for as we have seen, they were carried to every neighbouring sea-board by the hardy Scandinavian pirates.

All of them at first contained two elements, each of which had its own meaning, as in *Adalhard*, meaning noble, brave, from O.H. German *adal*, noble, and *hard*, brave, hard. This name which appears in the Domesday Book as *Adelardus* is the source of the modern surname *Adlard*.

Some of these elements are always used first in compounds ; others are employed finally. But the majority are used either first or last, as in the names *Winegær*, spear-friend, as in its opposite *Gærwine*, the source of the name of the famous editor and journalist, *J. L. Garvin*.

These elements are not very numerous and they recur again and again in different compounds.

Thus *Adal*, noble, already mentioned as an element of Adalhard (Adlard) occurs also in *Adalheim* and *Athelheim*. These mean noble protector from O. High German *adal*, noble, and *helm*, protector, helmet. These names yield the surnames *Adlam* and *Adlem*. *Allard* which is sometimes confused with *Adlard* is from *ealh*, temple, and *heard*, brave.

The surnames *Albert* and *Albright* are also from the same source and are modified forms of *Adalbrecht* and *Adalbert*. The second element is from *beorht*, bright, glorious.

The surname *Bert* is often a diminutive of Bertram or Herbert, but it is also the modern form of the Anglo-Saxon personal name *Beorht, Berht ;* while the second element in the Teutonic *Bertram*, glorious raven, is from *hram*, raven.

The names *Barrat, Barratt, Barret,* and *Berrett* are Teutonic in origin and come to us through the French *Barraud, Barrault,* and ultimately from the Teutonic *Berwalt*, bear-might. The four surnames are formed from the Teutonic name stem *Ber*, bear, with the French diminutives added.

Beorn which is Anglo-Saxon means warrior, noble, gives us with the addition of the diminutive *et*, the surnames *Barnet* and *Barnett*. As explained elsewhere these names like *Barrett* have other origins. Further confusion is caused by the O. Norse term *Bjorn*, from which the *Barnet* surnames are sometimes derived. For *bjorn* means bear, and the name is then an animal nickname.

The surname *Agar* is also of respectable antiquity, and means dread-army, from O. High German *agi*, *egi*, dread, and heri, army, while *Agibert* is dread-bright.

Aldwin is a less awe-inspiring name for it is from Anglo-Saxon *Ealdwine*, old friend ; from *ald*, old, and *wine*, friend.

Alfin has also a cheery sound and is from the Anglo-Saxon *ælf-wine*, fairy friend.

Alfred, the name of the famous King, is from Anglo-Saxon *Aelfred*, fairy counsel, from *ælf*, fairy, and *ræd*, counsel.

It should never be forgotten by students of Teutonic names that many of these came to us from the French, and that even where purely Anglo-Saxon names were concerned they were entered in the Rolls at a period when French was the official language of the country, and recorded by clerks, who though doubtless learned, and competent in other respects, had only an imperfect knowledge of the Early English dialects. In consequence of this they often gave one form to words of different origin and meaning. Thus there was much confusion between names, the first elements of which were *ælf*, fairy, and *ealh*, temple, and several surnames in *Al* or *El*. Of names which may definitely be regarded as originating in *Ealh*, temple, we may include *Allaway*, *Allcard*, and *Allchin*.

Allaway is a modern rendering of the Anglo-Saxon personal name *Alwy*, which is from *Ealwig*, and means temple-war, the second element *wig* meaning war or battle.

Alleard from Anglo-Saxon *Alhheard* from *ealh*, temple, and *heard*, brave.

Allchin, which sounds like a libellous nickname, is really a corruption of one of the most famous names in early history—*Alcuin* from *Alhwine*, temple-friend.

Another great name in Medieval history, that of *Anselm*, ecclesiastic and statesman, is Teutonic. It is from Old H. German *Anshelm*, and means divine-protector, from *ans*, a god, and *helm*, helmet, protector.

The surname *Archibald* which was brought to us by the French in the guise of *Archambault* is also of Teutonic origin and is from *Erconbald* or *Erchanbald*, precious-bold, from *erchan*, *precious*, and *bald*, bold.

In the Hundred Rolls appears the name Roger *Arketel*. From this form come the varied surnames *Arkell*, *Arkill*, *Arkle*, and *Arcoll*. These are unmistakably of Norse origin. In the *Landnamabok*, *Ketell* occurs repeatedly as a personal name, and is derived from the sacred *Cytel*, kettle or cauldron, which was used in the temple worship of the northmen, before the introduction of the Christian faith. In his *Words and Places* Canon Taylor states that of the few surnames in Iceland one of the four commonest is *Kettle*. It is also the first element in the place name *Kettlewell*.

To return to *Arketel* and its modern variants. These, as well as the surname *Kettle*, made famous by a popular novelist, are from the Scandinavian *Arketell*, a compound of O. Norse *ari*, eagle, and *Ketill*, kettle or cauldron. *Kell* and *Chettle* are also surnames from Kettle.

The popular surname *Arnold* comes to us through the French *Arnold* and *Arnaud* from the Teutonic *Arnhold* and is probably from Old Norse *arn*, eagle, and

some names, notable examples of which are *Wingood* from the Anglo-Saxon *Winegod*, and *Wimbolt* from *Winebeald*.

Although a proportion of Teutonic names have suffered little change in their transfer to our modern directories it would be hazardous to assume that they come to us directly from Anglo-Saxon sources. Saxon names were never popular after the Conquest. If they had been in popular use they would have been clipped, rhymed, and truncated and otherwise outraged in the never ending effort of adapting them to the changes in popular taste. But they suffered none of these things because they were ignored, and only a fractional minority paid them reverence, and took them as surnames in memory of days when Anglo-Saxon names were held in respect and honour.

As we have seen some of these Teutonic names have bequeathed us several surnames, while others have been changed in form. We find endings like *heard* changed to *ett*, *beald* to *ball ; here* to *er ; heard* to *ard ; weald* to *ell* and *vard ;* and *lac* to *lake.* Not great changes perhaps, but sufficient to show that the names of which they formed a part had been in popular use. As in nearly all cases hard usage spells corruption it is safe to assume that these Teutonic names have come to us through the French from the Frankish conquerors of Gaul.

CHAPTER XV

AMERICAN SURNAMES

THERE is no more thrilling story in World-history than that of the struggles and adventures of the European settlers who first gained a foothold on the mainland of North America. It has the lights and shadows of vivid drama, its war of passions, its moments of despair, its complete and triumphant finale. It is a story of sufferings patiently endured, of unflinching courage in the face of overwhelming odds, of a spirit that neither disaster nor misfortune could quench. These pioneers cleared the woods, bridged the streams, drained the swamps, and first essayed the mighty task of transforming this new Continent of primeval forests into a smiling prosperous land. They little guessed as they strove to wrest sustenance from an unfriendly soil that they were " building better than they knew," and that as instruments of Destiny they were settling the future of many millions yet unborn.

The story of the " Mayflower " and the New England settlements is familiar to all. Less is known of the struggles of the first colonists in Virginia.

After Sir Humphrey Gilbert's fruitless effort to form a settlement on the Atlantic coast, his brother-in-law, Sir Walter Raleigh, sailed for Virginia, but he and his followers were driven back to their ships by the native Indians.

While the fate of Raleigh's expedition hung in the balance the Venturers of London, Plymouth and Bristol co-operated in new schemes of colonisation. The expeditions that were the fruit of these plans met with partial success. The first venture of the Plymouth Company ended in misfortune, as Captain Pring and his ships were captured by the Spaniards. But this did not discourage the Company, for ship after ship followed with would-be colonists, eager to try their fortunes in the New World, and some hundreds were lodged in wooden shelters along the banks of the Sagadhoc River. Other settlements followed in the peninsula of Pemmequid and on the James River. The tide of immigration never ceased to flow. A succession of ships sailed up the James River bringing new colonists. By 1618 the country was considered safe enough for women to live there, and in that year a ship sailed to Virginia carrying ninety maids, and the Company offered special rewards to the men who would marry them.

Such offers were needless in that Eve-less wilderness, and all had the best of matrimonial opportunities.

With the granting of the Charter of Liberties, which was read out to the assembly of the settlers in the church at Jamestown in 1619, all doubt of the ultimate success of the new Dominions was at an end. But the goal of peace and prosperity was yet afar off. Attacks by the Indians, massacres, rebellions and other ills were endured before the way was made straight.

But Virginia was no longer a wilderness, and with every year that passed it became a more comfortable place of residence.

It is usual to find historians making the statement that emigration from England ceased from the middle of the seventeenth until towards the end of the eighteenth century. But the books of the Corporation of Bristol prove that at least ten thousand emigrants sailed for Virginia and Maryland from Bristol alone between 1654 and 1685. This list of Servants of the Plantations was published in 1929 and affords interesting information about early settlers in North America.

As is inevitable where large numbers are concerned these emigrants were of all sorts and conditions. A few were pardoned criminals; and a proportion political prisoners. There were few ages in English history when this resource ensured so constant a supply. Penruddock's rebellion in 1655 and the Scottish rising in 1666 furnished their share of emigrants. Many Cavaliers ruined by the Civil War sought shelter in this new home of the West. There were also a number of children and apprentices who were kidnapped and sold to the plantations. But the vast majority were respectable and industrious men and women, who bound themselves for a fixed term of service with the certainty of becoming freeholders at the end of that period. Many of these prospered exceedingly. Some became overseers for the great planters. But whatever their conditions, all found in the new land a greater measure of liberty than they had enjoyed at home.

These emigrants came from all parts of the United

Kingdom, though the majority appear to be English and Welsh. As in most lists of British names that of *Smith* far outnumbers all others, though those of *Davis, Jones, Williams, Thomas, Robinson, Hill, Edwards, Harris, James* and *Taylor* are of frequent occurrence.

Among occupative names we find *Cooke, Skinner, Gardener, Baker, Webbe, Walker, Tucker, Fowler, Wheeler, Archer, Shepherd, Painter, Turner, Pinder (Pounder), Butler, Cooper, Parker, Barker, Chapman, Belonger (Boulanger ?), Woodward, Goldsmith, Fisher, Brewer, Webster, Carter, Cutler, Salter, Glasier, Tanner, Cheesman, Glover, Singer, Merchant, Lockyer, Ward, Backster (Baxter), Clark, Carpenter, Spencer, Wright, Chaundler (Chandler), Hunter, Fletcher, Dyer, Vidler, (Fidler), Carrier, Day* (the old English name for farmworker), *Thatcher, Waterman, Bond* (meaning farmer, of which the compound is Husband), *Pavier, Piper, Boutcher* (Butcher), *Bricker* (Bridger), *Rodman* (from Anglo-Saxon *radman*, or tenant who held land in return for military service), *Fuller, Knight, Mercer, Palmer, Kingman* (means either King's servant or one under protection of royalty).

There are a multitude of patronymics in this list like *Philips, Griffiths, Bevan (ap Evan), Bowen (ap Owen), Stephens, Harry, Bennet, Batsson (Batson), Hix (Hicks), David, Collins* (from Nicholas), *Peters, Jefferis, James, Giles, Waters, Johnson, Hughes, Clements, Adams, Parry (ap Harry), Hanson, Gilbert, Willis, Ireson, Lewis, Richards, Rogers, Roger, Wilson, Allen, Dikson (Dickson), Powell (ap Howell), Andrewes, Charles, Roberts, Aphowell, Jobson, Harrison, Higgins,*

*Morgan, Jenkin, Tison, Jacob, Samuell (Samuel),
Pattison, Martin, Addams, Prosser (ap Rosser), Symons,
Price (ap Rice), Dodge, Jenings, Nicholas, Emson,
George, Evan, Mathewes, Rowland,* and *Tomlinson.* It
should be noted that the last of these names is also
sometimes local.

There is also an entry *Gibsin* which is obviously
meant for *Gibson.*

There are also several diminutive forms, the chief of
which are *Watkins, Jenkins, Adkins, Atkins, Hopkins,
Hancock, Hodgkins, Tompkins,* and *Poskins.*

Local names are also well represented. Among
them are *Wood, Moor, Ash, Horne, House, England,
Lisbon, Milton, Littleford, Huntington, Brooks,
Champnes, Hill, Langford, Hall, Callowhill, Whitehall,
Mainsbridge, Hayford, Wells, West, North, Dike,
Bristow, Whitehouse, Field, Grange, Northway, Danger-
field, Bolton, Twiford, Bradshaw, Church, Ashby, West-
bury, Farrington, Holbrooke, Shatford, Ford, Porch,
Tiverton, Bedford, Hampton, Land, Pool, Hedges,
Hayter* (High Tor), *Wootlane* (Woodlane ?), *Salisbury,
Underhill, Oxford, York, Orchard, Whitfield, White-
thorne, Eton, Attwood, Greenfield, Somerset, Whiteacre,
Lee, Godsell.*

Nicknames include : *Pope, Bishop, Drake, Duck,
Medcalfe* (Meadcalf), *Ferrett, Lord, Shin, Kidney,
Scarlett, Bullock, Fox, Lamb, Merry, Head, Dark,
Murray, Bliss, Veal, Green, Hart, Golden, Popejoy,
Camel, Crookshank, Moody, Beard, Sweet, Legg, Meek,
Whittle, White, Constant, Merryweather, Long, Short,
Salmon, Stout, Cotton, Poinard, Drinkwater, Lung,*

As we turn from the short and simple annals of American life in the seventeenth century, to that of the twentieth we find an amazing change and development. The small scattered companies of British, French, German, Dutch and Spanish settlers have been reinforced by many millions among whom are representatives of every race and nation, and the United States of America have been principally recruited from the disunited States of Europe. Only a minority of American citizens—a minority that shrinks year by year to smaller proportions—regard England as their mother country. As H. L. Mencken says in that excellent and illuminating work, *The American Language :*

" The Germans . . . pre-empted the best lands East of the mountains before the new republic was born. And so in our own time we have seen the Swedes and Norwegians shouldering the native from the wheat lands of the North, West, and the Italians driving the decadent New Englanders from their farms, and the Jews gobbling New York, and the Sclavs getting a firm foot-hold in the mining regions, and the French Canadians penetrating New Hampshire and Vermont, . . . and the awakened negroes gradually ousting the whites from the farms of the South."

For more than two centuries this human tide has flowed ceaselessly and steadily from the Eastern to the Western Hemisphere, an exodus of such dimensions and amazing staying power is without parallel in World History. One of the results of this change-over is that America offers a fuller and more varied list of surnames than any other nation. Itself a composite of nearly every race, it has taken many surnames from each. A short study of the City Directories of New York, Boston, Chicago, Pittsburg or San Francisco discloses the names of Germans, Swedes, Armenians, Hungarians, Greeks, Spaniards, Italians, Frenchmen, Dutch, Jews and Sclavs, as well as those of the earlier British settlers. Thus we find names like *Schmidt*, *Meyer*, *Fuchs*, *Hoffman*, *Lucker*, *Schneider*, *Mlinar*, *Zadek*, *Lopez*, *Olson*, *La Ferge*, *Voight*, *De Camp*, *Henri*, *Crago*, *Hernandez*, *Svennigsen*, *Pungi*, *Klok*, *Jurk*, *App*, *Cortissoz*, *Carlsen*, and *Zapinkow*.

Murphy, which figured as *Murfey* in the List of Stuart times is very strongly represented in the Directories of New York and other American cities where Irish people are gathered in force. In New York it is the fourth most common name. Other Irish names that approach it in popularity are *Sullivan*, *O'Brien*, *Ryan*, and *Donnelley*.

In the Directories of New York, Boston and Chicago there are hosts of English or Scottish names like *Arnold*, *Lynn*, *Wood*, *Mudie*, *Adkins*, *Twigg*, *Aldrich*, *Ashwin*, *Andrews*, *Bacon*, *Baker*, *Banks*, *Bartlett*, *Billing*, *Bishop*, *Blunt*, *Brewer*, *Brown*, *Buchanan*, *Butterfield*, *Carpenter*, *Chapman*, *Elmes*, *Winter*, *Young*, *Watson*, *Wolf*, *Tanner*, *Smart*, *Long*, *Laird*, *Judd*, *Glover*, *Williams*, *Good*, *Wilson*, *Budd*, *Campbell*, *Cobb*, *Drury* and *Myers*, to mention only a few.

Most of these have already been discussed in previous chapters, and some of them are of quite respectable ancestry. *Arnold* is of Low German origin, but sometimes it is derived from the place name Arnold.

Wood is generally local (at the wood) but often as old records show it was used to nickname one who was regarded as mad or violent. Here the Anglo-Saxon word *wód* was called into service. Sometimes a more fully descriptive name was used and the unfortunate was called, as we find in the Hundred Rolls, *Badintheheved*. Even in these enlightened days those whose intellectual endowments are not particularly manifest are often objects of ridicule to their neighbours especially when these belong to opposite parties or factions.

Mudie is the Scottish form of *Moody* which in its turn means the valiant and bold. *Adkins* is a diminutive of *Adam*. *Twigg* is one of those curious nicknames which medieval people gave their friends out of sheer caprice.

Ashwin is a Teutonic name from *Æscwine*, *ash* (*spear*)—*friend*. *Andrews* is a simple patronymic that requires no explanation. *Billing* is pure Anglo-Saxon ; *Laird*, a Scottish form of *Lord* ; *Eddy*, a pet form of Edward ; *Myers* is a local name and indicates its owner's address—at the mire. But its popularity as a surname is not due to this source alone. For it has been much mixed up with sundry names like Mayer and Mair. It also, as Professor Weekley points out, sometimes represents *mire*, the old French term for a physician. In addition to this it should be noted that many *German Meyers* who settled in England and America found *Myers* a convenient name to adopt.

In the Introductory chapter it was shown that in Great Britain a few names are found in all counties and districts, and that others enjoy special popularity in some regions and are scarcely represented in others. It was also demonstrated that while *Smith*, the commonest of English surnames, is borne by one in every eighty-eight of the inhabitants of Glasgow, and one in fifty of the people of Edinburgh, it shows a remarkable shrinkage in other Scottish towns. In Wales also there are parishes where a majority of the inhabitants answer to the name of *Jones*.

In the United States there is a similar unevenness of distribution in surnames. Here the commoner English names yield pride of place to Irish, Jewish and German names, though in the principal cities *Smith* still heads the lists. But this statement, however, requires some qualification, for as Mr. Mencken points out, " there are whole regions in the South West in which *Lopez* and *Gonzales* are far commoner names than *Smith*, *Brown* or *Jones*, and whole regions in the Middle West wherein *Olson* is commoner than either *Taylor* or *Williams*, and places both North and South where *Duval* is at least as common as *Brown*."

Mr. Mencken also states that among the commoner names in New York the fourth and fifth places are held by *Murphy* and *Meyer* and that after these come *Schultz* and *Kraus*, while among the fifty commonest are *Schmidt*, *Muller*, *Schneider*, and *Klein*.

Meyer, farmer, is Germany's most popular name, and it has many compounds in the Fatherland. In the Reformation period some of the more snobbish owners of the name adopted the Latin equivalent *Agricola*, to distinguish them from the vulgar herd, but this form has not crossed the Atlantic.

Schultz is for local magistrate or judge. The adjective *Kraus*, curly or crisp, appears in compounds. In its simpler form it is a common surname in both Germany and America. Numerous as the *Schmidts*, *Mullers*, *Schneiders* and *Kleins* are they would be much more numerous still in many parts of the United States if many of the bearers of these names had not adopted English equivalents for them and become *Smiths*, *Millers*, *Taylor* and *Littles*. It is undoubtedly on this account that *Smith* stands first among the surnames of New York and that *Miller* holds the third place. *Brown*, which is second, has also been reinforced by many German *Brauns*. It was stated by the Bureau of War Risk Insurance (U.S.) in 1918 that there were then 15,000 Millers in the United States Army. Many of these, as Mr. Mencken rightly suggests, were originally Scandinavians who acknowledged the surname Moller, while the Polish *Jaunszewski* suffered a sea-change and has also become *Miller*. Even the Bohemian *Mlinar*, which looks like a Metathetic variation of the English *Milner*, contributes its quota to the Miller family.

Though many immigrants readily adopted English translations of their surnames, others, through ignorance or obstinacy, clung to their foreign ones, with the result that these were strangely mangled or corrupted. Thus the French *Petit* became *Poteet*, *Dejean* was changed to *Deshong*, and *Saule* to *Sewell*.

The Dutch *Van Huys* became *Vaunice*, *Reiger* was corrupted to *Rikes* and *Wörth* to *Wirt*.

Bunker's Hill of historic memory owes its name to a doughty warrior called *Bunker*, whose real name was *Bon Cœur*.

Compounds of the French *bon* are found in American directories though many of these retain their original spelling as in *Bonneau*, *Bonnard*, *Bonneteau*. *Bonney* and *Bonnet* are also common in Northern cities.

Berger, the French *Shepherd*, is also a common name in the States. Its diminutive *Bergeron* is also to be met with. The French *Dupuy* has become the American *Depew*.

The local name *Lasalle*, the hall, which is the same in meaning as the English *Sale* or *Hall*, flourishes unaltered side by side with these native forms.

Among patronymics we find names with the Teutonic affix *sen*, the German *sohn* as well as the English *son*. Sometimes we find in the same Directory examples of two or more of these endings being used with the same name, as in *Peterson* and *Petersen*, *Hanson* and *Hansen*, *Anderson* and *Andersen*, *Carlson* and *Carlsen*. The German *Stein* and the English *Stone*, like *Zimmerman* and *Carpenter*, rub elbows with each other in lists of traders. The shortened form *Zimmer* which in German means " room," is also common. We find some names variously spelt as in *Cooperman* and *Kooperman*.

Anderbrugg, which like *Vorderbrugg*, is a local surname that takes in both the preposition and the article, is found in the Chicago and other Directories.

17

In these there also appears that Teutonic dithemitic name Eberhardt, boar strong, that first was worn by some of those fierce self-reliant warriors of the North who terrorised Europe in the early centuries of the Christian era.

The American lists also show *Faunt*, the aphetic form of *enfaunt*—which as readers are aware crossed the English channel from France,—as well as *Kind* and *Knabe*, the German terms for child and boy.

Strangely enough we meet in the States money nicknames like *Shilling* and *Sovereign*, though neither of the coins indicated by these terms are in circulation in America. But the second of these can scarcely have reference to money, as the sovereign came into use long after English surnames were stabilised.

Cohen or *Colna*, the commonest of Jewish names, flourishes wherever members of the ancient faith are found, and is as well known in New York as London. It is a name of great antiquity and is found in Phœnician inscriptions as the official name of the priest. According to Hasting's Bible Dictionary (1867) the corresponding word in Arabic, *Kâhin*, means soothsayer. Hyamson, in his book on Jewish Surnames says of this surname, " Cohen, a tribal as much as a official name has known many variations. In Italy it is met with under the guise of *Sacerdote*. Other forms are *Acohen, Coen, Cohn, Cahen, Cahn, Kahn*."

Many of the Jewish names that were conferred at the close of the eighteenth century by the German and Austrian authorities like *Eselhaupt*, asses' head ;

Kohlkopf, cabbage-head, or blockhead ; *Susskind*, sweet-child ; *Zentnerschwer*, hundredweight-heavy ; *Kirschrot*, cherry-red ; *Himmelblau*, sky-blue ; *Kanalgeruch*, canal-smell ; *Küsse-mich*, kiss-me ; *Muttermilch*, mother's-milk ; *Temperaturwechsel*, change-of-temperature ; and other atrocities that disclose a heavy type of German humour were abandoned by immigrants on their arrival in America and surnames like *Cohen* or *Isaac* substituted for them.

In his book on the Huguenots, Samuel Smiles gives some account of the refugees who fled to America after the Revocation of the Edict of Nantes. This emigration was on a larger scale than is generally realised by historians. Among the first of the persecuted people to arrive was a company of Walloons who settled on Statue Island, and built a little church near Richmond. Afterwards they removed to a locality now known as Wallabout, a corruption of the old name *Wahle Bocht* or the Bay of Foreigners. Until recent years the *Grisons* and *Disoways*, descendants of these immigrants occupied the farms that their ancestors first tilled two centuries ago. There were two settlements in the State of New York, one at Albany, and the other at Manhattan. At the latter the Walloons were joined by a company of Vaudois from the South of France. Huguenots hunted from France also found homes in New Rochelle and Westchester County. From these emigrants have descended men like *Jay* and *de Lancey* whose names recall notable events in American history.

In Massachusetts many Huguenots found a spiritual home, and it should not be forgotten that the historic

Faneuil Hall, where the demand for independence was so often heard in pre-Revolution days, was the gift of the son of one of these French refugees.

More than one thousand Huguenots settled in South Carolina who fled there via Holland. Three colonies were formed at Charleston, and the first pastor of the Huguenot church there was Elias *Prioleau*, a lineal descendant of Antoine *Prióli* who was Doge of Venice in 1618. These French settlers made some notable contributions to the Roll of American surnames ; for among them we find those of *Perronneau, Ravenel, Laurens, Fravezant, Neuville, Boudinot, Manigault, Marion, Legare, Huger, Gaillard, Benort, Bayard, Dupré,* and *Chevalier*.

In Virginia also there were Huguenot settlements, and from the families of Maury and Fontaine, who were the leaders of these exiles, have descended several illustrious men, who have added to the renown of the land of their adoption.

History repeats itself, in the changes and influences that overtake names and words, as in the arena of world affairs. And just as in the seventeenth century the names of Huguenot refugees were changed from *Villebois* to *Williamise*, *Le Coq* to *Laycock*, *Drouet* to *Drewitt*, *D'Orleans* to *Darling* and *Taillebois* to *Talboys*, so for more than a century a similar transformation has been going on, and still continues.

But today the problem is infinitely more complicated than it was in the earlier centuries. Every year the young Republic of the West stretches out giant arms and draws in an army of new citizens, from every continent and country. These people of every race and class must of necessity conform to the institutions and customs of the land of their adoption, and one of the first things many of these citizens do, so as to facilitate intercourse with others, is to take a name that sounds familiar to American ears.

As Mr. Mencken shows in *The American Language* this process goes on quietly but continuously ; and so we see, as he says *Bloch* changed to *Block* or *Black*, *Huber* to *Hoover*, *Kempf* to *Kemp*, *Kerngut* to *Kerngood*, *Betz* to *Betts*, *Jung* to *Young*, *Loeb* to *Lobe*, the Dutch *Broywer* to *Brower*, *Hoogsteen* to *Highstone*, *Veldhuis* to *Fieldhouse*. By the same process the Greek *Triantafyllopoulos* (meaning rose) becomes *Rose*, and *Giannopoulos*, *Johnson*. Similarly the Polish *Wilkie-wiez* is changed to *Wilson*, and the Bohemian *Kovár* becomes *Smith*.

Many names are translations as in the change over from *König* to *King*, *Weissberg* to *Whitehill*, *Steiner* to *Stoner*, *Meister* to *Master*, *Morgenstern* to *Morningstar*, *Vogelgesang* to *Birdsong*, *Schwartz* to *Black*, and *Stern* to *Starr*.

For about eight centuries England has been a place of refuge for the exile, yet there are relatively only a few foreign names in English Directories. In the American Directories there are almost as many foreign as English names, which is easy to understand, when we remember that there immigration is almost continuous. In England two or three generations passed before the immigrant regarded himself as a native. In America the change-over is more quickly effected.

The same transformation is going on in America, and in time those who bear names that proclaim their owners as foreigners will become plain Smiths, Millers or Browns. But until immigration ceases this foreign element will continue to exercise its influence and proclaim its presence in American name lists.

INDEX

263

18